Jacques Seray

1904

The Tour de France which was to be the last

By the same author:

To the Beautiful Signs
(Edisud, 1992)

Two Wheels, The Veritable History of the Velo
(Editions du Rouergue, 1988)

In collaboration with Jean Durry:
The 100 Most Beautiful Routes for Cyclotourism
(Denoel, 1984)

To be published:
The Beautiful Public Clock

ISBN 0-9649835-2-4 (English Edition)
Translation from the French provided by Richard Yates.
Worldwide English rights held by Buonpane Publications,
a division of Colorado Creative Media, Inc.
P.O. Box 40724, Denver, CO 80204. 303 831 0917.
Distributed in Great Britain by Bromely Books for Sport & Publicity.
(011) 0171 794 0915

ISBN 2-9508500-0-6 (French Edition)
© Jacques Seray, 1994.
8, allée de Normandie,
78140 Vélizy-Villacoublay, France

Table of Contents

1904 Tour de France Route

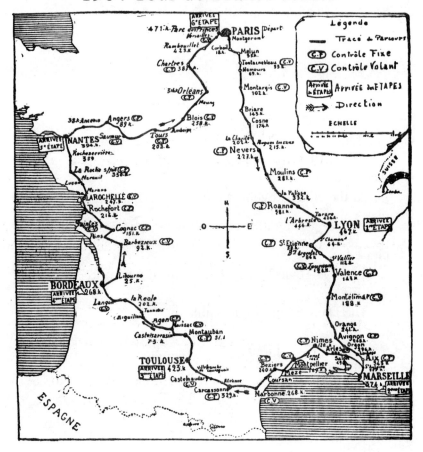

Chapter One
At the House of Desgrange

The tram accelerated away with the wheels grinding against the rails. It was, however, a very modern machine in that it was electric. Georges Abran preferred it to the underground railway, the Metropolitan. Tunnels, he did not like. And this "Metro," about which everyone was talking so much, still did not go everywhere you wanted to go. Although he was not really keen on this type of progress, he had to admit that an underground railway in the center of Paris was really something. In this year 1904, problems with traffic were unavoidable, with the carriages, the trams, the buses which ran on muscles and hay, and now with the motorcars. Would this "Metropolitan" born with the new century surmount them?

In the tram, Georges Abran chose a seat away from the other passengers. A lady came and sat down opposite him. He moved back to the very edge of his seat so that she could get past with her wide dress. She lifted the skirt so that it did not trail on the floor. A large violet on her wide-brimmed hat partly hid her face. "A Bourgeoisie," he said to himself. For his part, he preferred a style which delighted his tailor. He liked well-cut suits, broad-brimmed hats and white shirts but always worn with a bow tie. This attribute was certainly very much the fashion but, he intended that his own carried his personal touch. It must be as striking as possible and really stand out from his jacket.

With much squealing, the tram came to a stop. "Montmartre Station." Not the famous hill of Montmartre which looked down on Paris from the north side of the city but that of Faubourg (lower) Montmartre. It was the Montmartre of a thousand occupations, of industry, of business and of pleasure. If Paris was multifarious, this is where one if its hearts beat.

Abran stepped onto the pavement. Lost in thought, he nearly collided with a laundry maid. On her head she carried a wicker basket. She was walking carefully because she was obliged to steady her load with one hand and lift her long skirt with the other. The man who made her jump was the object of her indignation. As he excused himself Abran quickly ran his eye over her. In spite of the apron which covered her skirt, she was unrumpled, with her hair neatly tied into a bun and was wearing a blouse with short, gathered sleeves and a low-cut neckline. As he reflectively stroked his short white beard he realized that at his age it would be foolish to be too gallant in this situation.

The sun shone. What terrible traffic! Abran strolled on, reflecting on the life of the street. He always enjoyed the area even though he knew it so well. Look, a motorcar. A Cotterreau. Recently he had become interested in this make which owed its name to a former racing cyclist. The vehicle was caught up in the maelstrom of the boulevard. For the moment it was stuck behind an omnibus. The driver cursed. This rather amused some of the passengers on the top deck. At last the conductor with his hat well screwed onto his head and his satchel wrapped across his shoulders gave the signal to start. The driver cracked his whip and the three horses attached to the bus slowly pulled away and the traffic began to move again. Soon the Cottereau and other motorcars would no longer have to progress over horse droppings. Another sign of progress. Cobblestones had been laid in the road, this was the best way of doing away with the dust which was thrown up by the traffic. The dust was the worst scourge of the streets of Paris. Even though they were well watered every morning, the benefit was only temporary. There was much talk of asphalt or more economically using a product invented by a certain Mr. de Westrum which consisted of tar emulsified with water, but these things never seemed to get further than the planning stage.

The man with the wide bow tie turned onto the Rue du Faubourg Montmartre. What a lot of people. He stepped out of the way of a coalman staggering under the weight of a sack of anthracite. He did not look like a salesman, like one of those who "went to the coal" once a week to prove they had a job. The expression had always amused Abran: "going to the coal."

6

Here was number 10. He went through an archway. An earth courtyard[1]. On the left, some small workshops and, on the right, a bare wall. At the end, a neat and tidy facade even though it saw little sun. The man with the beard made a mental note that the building had not deteriorated too much in the four years that he had known it. He remembered it well. It was the time of *L'Auto-Velo*, the name then given to the newspaper where he was already working. The title had changed, in order to become simply *L'Auto*. A court case had ruled that the owner was obliged to modify the original name. The reason? Another sporting daily, *Le Velo*, which had been founded in 1892 struck back, considering that it was a direct competitor. There was no room for two of them when it came to singing the praises of glory achieved by muscle power. Anyway it was the ambition of *L'Auto-Velo* to corner the market. The number one in the field, the pugnacious Pierre Giffard fiercely defended the title to which he thought he had the right. So any change in the situation would only take place with the greatest of difficulty. It was necessary to give way. For the time being, for they were committed to battle and the knives began to come out.

At the time, Abran remembered, they had only taken possession of the second floor. The floors above were taken up by other occupants: a supplier of feathers and flowers to decorate ladies' hats, a photographer who stopped only at going to a convent to obtain his models, and several rather bourgeois households. The first floor was not yet devoted to the press. It was at the time of the change of the paper's title that he had been appointed. The change proved to be the catalyst of a new dynamic for the company.

The man with the bow tie suddenly abandoned his thoughts as he caught sight of a young man. It was one of his friends. His name was Géo Lefèvre. He was a journalist with a talented pen. He was coming down the sole staircase of the building. In fact, there was a single ramp which connected all the floors together, the editor's office, the workshops and... ˝the holy of holies.˝[2]

"Is Bostock here?" he asked.

"He must be in his office somewhere. He might even have slept here last night."

"Bostock." The curious name had come from the lips of the man with the white beard. He could have said "the boss" or even "Desgrange," since it was he to whom he was referring. He preferred this nickname taken from a lion tamer currently app earing in Paris. For more than a year, he had only referred to the editor of *L'Auto* by this sobriquet. It dated from the period when Desgrange wanted to strike a blow against his competitors and was racking his brains to find a method to do so. His staff, who were often the recipients of his ire, had to face the fact that he had become nearly unapproachable. His fight with *Le Velo* had made him short-tempered. It was never contemplated by the owners of the newspaper to modify his offensive spirit.

Undoubtedly, there were many memories running through the mind of the man with the white beard today. The image of Desgrange was taking a prominent place. What a fighter! Even back in 1901 had he not already made a big impact in the field of sporting contests. His idea? To repeat the famous cycling race Paris-Brest-Paris disputed over 1200 kilometers in one stage, as had been done ten years previously. The event - curiously enough - had been created by Pierre Giffard, the then chief editor of the *Petit Journal*, the most important French newspaper. And this relaunch had been enormously successful. It was Maurice Garin who had written his name in golden letters in the record book, following in the footsteps of the famous Charles Terront, nicknamed "The Man," and which paradoxically made him into a god. But, as it had been decided as a mark of respect to this monument of cycling to only organize the event every ten years, something else had to be quickly found to please the readers, to assure and even augment the sales of *L'Auto*. The paper in general, and Desgrange in particular, tended to favor another cycling race. For the double reason that the latter stemmed from the world of bicycling and that this sport seemed to be the only thing able to produce its own heroic act to attract the public.

In 1902, Abran remembered, they also ran a Marseille-Paris race. It was a very good event. To this Desgrange blatantly added a Bordeaux-Paris, it was a duplicate - and provocatively advertised - of the event run by his rival *Le Velo*. A race which made respectable profits was always of interest to the cashier of *L'Auto*. Imagine, two Bordeaux-Paris in the same year.[3] It was then that Géo Lefèvre, the man who Georges Abran had just passed on the stairs, suggested to Desgrange to raise the stakes. Why not launch the riders on a tour of the whole of France? The idea appeared to be somewhat unrealistic. Just imagine the responsibilities and risks. And even the incredible amount of work involved just to get it off the ground. When the idea was first proposed, it was met with a hesitant and then a negative response. But after thinking it over they slowly came round to the idea. In the eyes of the men of the press the idea was seen as a tremendous "soap opera" which would last for three weeks. The event would create its own story. And that would be a sales factor.

The face of the man with the large bow tie lit up and he smiled. He relived the scene when Desgrange appointed him "The Delegate of *L'Auto*," charged with making various necessary contacts. His main task. To go over the route, to make all the material arrangements, and then when the great day finally came, follow the event and act as the official representative of *L'Auto*, everywhere that it was necessary.

The second floor. Abran was in front of Desgrange's office. The door was not closed. He knocked on it all the same.

"Come in," he heard. "Sit down, Abran."

"Good morning Gustave."

Everyone outside the inner circle would be surprised by this, for Desgrange's Christian name was Henri. Abran did indeed astonish his small world with the fanciful names he gave to his boss. Desgrange was perfectly at ease with this type of levity and always took it in good humor. It was the sign of a certain intimacy between the two men.

Before Abran was able to make even the most minor remark such as inquiring into the state of health of his director, Desgrange-Bostock-Gustave dispensed with the polite chatter.

"So, tell me about your trip. Is everything ready? The flying controls, the fixed controls, the stages? Is everybody ready? During all your meetings, did you see Doctor Thomas at Agen? And Louis Bonneville, at Toulouse? They're good men, they are. I always remember the work they did for the U.V.F."[4]

"Yes everything is ready. I certainly saw your friends. Albert Thomas is even giving a 'prime,' (a prize during for a stage win) in memory of the time when he was the president of the Union."

"He is doing me a great honor. You see, Abran, I have very fond memories of that period, the hesitant beginning of cycle sport. You who are older than I am, no doubt you remember the fervor for the bicycle which ran through every level of society. It's no longer the case these days. In ten years a lot of things have happened. The bicycle has been abandoned by the wealthy classes. It's a very good thing that people like Thomas and Bonneville have remained faithful and bring back the memory of those mad years."

Abran's gaze was fixed on the face of Desgrange. It was true that he was younger than him. His beard had not yet become white. But Georges could not dwell on this reflection, his boss was waiting for his report.

"Leon Breton and Raoul d'Arnaud, the actual directors of the U.V.F. have a rather different view. You remember, Gustave, when you went to see them last year to tell them about the birth of the Tour de France. They were hardly enthusiastic. They advised you against even attempting this adventure."

"That's true. And Paul Rousseau,[5] their colleague, judge and judged himself because being associated with Le Velo, he had difficulty in hiding the fact that he was opposed to the whole idea. However, he's still a friend. But, Abran, tell me about your survey? What is radically new since last year?"

"The idea of the Tour has caught on, contacts are much easier. At Toulouse I was welcomed with open arms. At Marseille, less so, those in charge did not seem well disposed. I hope we won't have any problems with them and that everything will be all right at the Larcheveque velodrome. But, generally speaking, what worries me most is the state of the roads. Once again the riders are going to be 'eating dust.'"

"I deplore it too, Abran. But what can you do? Do you know what my major worry is? It's the list of starters. It's a poor one. I would never be able to say so publicly but, between you and me, the whole field contains only two real riders, Maurice Garin and Hippolyte Aucouturier. Those who would be able to legitimately compete with them, the Petit-Bretons and the Georgets are blossoming on the track. They prefer to battle it out in the Bol d'Or.[6] We need them, Abran. We must convince them. But, as I know, it's a question of money. For this year we'll have to get the public to focus their attention on the match between Garin and Aucouturier. You know the tactic used to publicize an event by building up the rivalry between the competitors? I have in the past condemned those who have organized track meetings and exaggerated the antagonism between two opponents. But this year, we have no choice. Let's hope it will be a good fight and the results will be in doubt for most of the race. Let's hope that Géo will know how to boost it up!"

"You can be sure he will."

This Géo, the firm's other Georges, the one that Abran had just met in the building, was Géo Lefèvre. A robust man who had been entrusted with a job that was much more than that of a mere journalist. He also had to follow the event and keep a strict eye on the sporting aspect. Although he was not one of the race commissioners he had to make sure the rules were observed. A heavy burden for a man of only twenty-eight years.

Desgrange continued, "I am not suggesting Georges, that you can do anything about the poor list of starters we have."

Desgrange sometimes called Abran by his Christian name. He really had to when the other addressed him as "Gustave."

"The prizes." Abran replied.

"Yes, the prizes are allocated. We're short of money. Last year's rampant generosity cannot be repeated this year. The remuneration has practically been cut in half. And obviously, this is all the champions notice. However, what about the start at Montgeron?"

"Everything is ready there. The Hotel Reveil-Matin will be on a war footing. According to the rumors, there will be no shortage of spectators in the area."

"This year, Abran, for lack of stars, we'll have a fine regular race. Regular because there will be no pacers. The pacers create a real gap between the champions and the others. The lesser-known ones do not have the means to afford them. Under the new rules, I've made another sweeping change. From now on help during the race is forbidden outside the controls. I believe these changes will make a lot of difference. Are you familiar with the new rules, Georges?"

"Yes, I've studied them closely."

Abran, whose main strength was his steadfastness, replied without hesitating. To show that he was fully conversant with the rules, he pulled from his leather briefcase several typed sheets of paper. Desgrange, who never wasted a moment of his time, used the opportunity to open his mail.

This rule was a complete break from the past. In its articles 6 to 8, pacers were forbidden.[7] Nonetheless no one could be accused of authoritarianism. Its sole objective was the uniformity of the event. Since 1891, the year which saw the beginning of the great road races in France, pacers had been permitted. Charles Terront had not been deprived of them in the initial Paris-Brest-Paris. And, ten years later, Maurice Garin, in the second edition, had gotten it down to a fine art. While he already had a robust team at his disposal, he was also able to recruit those of his teammate Constant Huret who had retired. So the best rider of them all had no need to fear feeling the wind on his nose. It was all perfectly legal and there was no question of straying from the rules. But suspicion was beginning to arise from the actions of some following vehicles during the night hours. When the riders were isolated and financial interests were at stake, it was possible that some of them would bend their code of ethics.

It was in order to avoid this risk of cheating that "secret" controls were brought in. Their main strength was obviously that by their very nature their locations were impossible to predict. They completed the battery of "fixed" and "flying" controls.

All these mandatory halts were significant in other ways. For the cyclists there was the opportunity to eat more copiously than they could while riding, to take on provisions and, sometimes, to attend to mechanical problems. For the organizers it was a way of breaking up the stage and to make a note of the passage of the riders. But, it was also an opportunity to attract the spectators who would be able to touch their idols. And, in this way, to reinforce the right image of the Tour de France, which would be, of course associated with L'Auto.

It must be said that with *L'Auto* there were no half-measures when it came to extolling the virtues of the champions. The journalists never hesitated to push lyricism to its limits. Their latest trick consisted of elevating the stars to a new level of supremacy. They were "demi-gods." A new mythology was born. So the question was posed, "Are these beings who draw their strength from another, better world, are they really made of flesh and blood? Do they ooze the same sweat as the common man?"

Desgrange was one of the first to indulge in this special style of journalism. Towards the end of his career he admitted that, "We made the sport on the road overly ornate in the same way as the poets of the 17th Century gilded the lily of love."

Géo Lefèvre played his part in the process. And as he was not short of talent, his inspiration often ran over the yellow pages of *L'Auto*. The most recent example of his excess was in that day's paper.

"Tomorrow at nine o'clock in the evening, the competitors of the 1904 Tour de France will commence their effort, and in only 23 days we will see them, one by one, exhausted and covered with dust, return to the Paris which they left together in one big bunch, with a big hope in their hearts and in their bodies a supply of energy to be expended over the entire length of 2,400 kilometers of the route.

"Very soon they are going to disappear into the tunnel of the night and they will emerge from it as the sun rises, at noon they will begin to roast, then, perhaps, they will be condemned to struggle in the rain and against a wind unleashed into a tempest, and all the great regions of France will successively see their passing, bowed down to their task, struggling grimly, and thinking only of their far-off goal which draws ever nearer with every stroke of the pedals.

"The green of the Nievre region, the abrupt heights of the Col de la Republique, the white roads of Provence, the ruins of Arles and of Nimes, the pink buildings of Toulouse, the slopes of the Bordeaux vineyards, the Atlantic with its silvery sparkle, they will slowly leave them all behind under the astonished looks of the peasants and the villagers, this will all be accomplished with neither truce nor rest.

"Imagine for an instant the magnitude of the task to which these wonderful roadmen have submitted themselves and you will certainly remain convinced that these men are of another flesh, of another blood than we are, and you too will admit that human energy knows no limits."

It was, in fact, the day before the great start. And Georges Abran had come to receive his final orders. His role was simple. Now that he knew everything was in place on the road, it only remained for him to officiate as the starter. Like all those who are charged with releasing the competitors, he must point his pistol to the sky. But in his case he is also obliged to wave a yellow flag, the banner of *L'Auto*. His solemn mission was to demonstrate his authority when the riders are called and to "throw them" to the public. In brief, he was to represent *L'Auto* and personify its virtues.

Desgrange resumed the dialogue. "I saw Aucouturier yesterday, he came with his manager Alibert. His ambition is obvious. 'The Terrible' wants to win!"

Abran took note of the employment of this nickname. For Desgrange to use it was not surprising. It was perhaps he who invented it in the first place. In any case, the more this type of term appeared in the columns of *L'Auto*, the more readers there were!

Desgrange continued, "We are going to enlarge on the vindictive feelings of Aucouturier. Géo is taking care of it. We are going to concentrate on only two of the stars, we must emphasize their differences."

"And Garin?"

"No problem. Although he registered his name a long time ago, he wrote to us to announce his participation."

"He wrote to us?"

"Don't be stupid, Georges. Read *L'Auto* tomorrow. You'll find the essential information there."

Undoubtedly, Abran was obliged to recognize that he was working with the very best in the business. The next day, the first of July, *L'Auto* published the following letter.

> "Paris, 29th June, 1904
>
> Dear Sir,
>
> I return to Paris, quite ready, in good form and ready for the struggle. I have been preparing over the route between Paris and Marseille, my portions and my potions. It only remains for me to swallow them.
>
> I remain, etc.
>
> Maurice Garin"

Like every reader, Abran also looked at the map of the route. But he learned nothing from this. He was the route, it was his work. Paris, Lyon, Marseille, Toulouse, Bordeaux, Nantes and Paris again. He knew them all. The volunteers who would run the controls, he could describe their features and imitate their accents. He knew every part of them. A man from Lyons was nothing like a man from Marseille. A man from Marseille was nothing like a man from Toulouse. Someone from Toulouse had nothing in common with one from Bordeaux. And do you really believe that if you come from Nantes you are anything like a Parisian? Abran knew all these men, he was a great traveller. His close friends called him the "Wandering Jew." In the nicest possible way.

A man who enjoyed the good things of life, Abran, was also a good and efficient employee. His journalistic friends sometimes laughed at him with his white beard, his broad-brimmed hat and his big bow ties. But what did they really understand about him? They could not even be sure if his mode of dress was classic or extravagant. He had chosen a certain lifestyle and made it his own. Géo Lefèvre, who was young enough to be his son, gently made fun of him. Sometimes he even flayed him, accusing him of being short-winded and fueled by 'Pernod'. Just because his breath sometimes smelled of anise seed. What do you expect, a man of his age needs to be fortified. Now a man such as he, a starter, has no need of abstinence, he does not draw his salary directly from the practice of riding a bicycle but by other means.

----

1 It would be many more years before the courtyard of *L'Auto* was to be paved. There were also rails laid down to facilitate the delivery of the spools of paper which fed the presses.

2 Later, this modest ramp was to become such a superb staircase that a preservation order was placed on it.

3 It is one of the great ironies of the sport that this event has disappeared from the calendar of the professional races.

4 Union Velocipedique de France, the national cycling federation.

5 Leon Breton and Paul Rousseau had for several decades occupied the posts as major executives.

6 The Bol d'Or was a famous track race run in the Buffalo Velodrome, located in Neilly, in the southeast of Paris.

7 Article 6 - The event will be run with neither pacers, nor followers, nor helpers of any sort.

"By this it must be understood that a rider will not be reproached for: (i) finding himself alongside a curious spectator on a bicycle;

(ii) from accepting a little food or a drink from a cyclist or a passerby; (iii) from even exchanging his machine with one lent to him by an unknown cyclist of good will; (iv) to dismount to eat or even be seen to be doing so; on the contrary, any competitor receiving any aid whatsoever on the road, be it from a pacer, a helper, or a follower in the service of the rider or in the service of the manufacturer whose machine he is riding, will be immediately disqualified from the race.

"On the other hand, the competitors have the right, at the controls, to have helpers and spare machines; they can also have spare machines in the different towns along the route which have no controls."

Article 7 - Vehicles and motorcars are formally forbidden. It is obvious that the organizers of the 'Tour de France' cannot prevent all motor vehicles from following the race but all riders who have a following car at their disposal containing, for example, provisions, spare bicycles, pacers, will be disqualified from the race.

Article 8 - Changes of bicycles are authorized. The entire route must be covered by the rider without leaving his bicycle even on the climbs when he is obliged to walk. The rider must be helped by no one."

Chapter 2
At the Reveil-Matin

When the little man in the white jacket made his appearance, shivers ran through the crowd, "The Little Chimney Sweep!"

This nickname sat well on Maurice Garin. He was well past his thirty-third birthday, and he was still known by the appellation given to him at the very beginning of his career. But if it amused him, it was also a measure of his popularity. Ten years previously, a journalist, having discovered that he was born in Italy in the valley of Aosta, which, like Savoy furnished Lyon and Paris with those who scraped chimneys, gave him this nickname. A caricaturist had even sketched him with a blackened face and a long-handled brush in his hand. The image stuck. But it was true that he was not very tall, our energetic Maurice. In rather a caustic manner, he was also called "The Italian." Preferably when he was beaten. Even though he had lived in Lens for most of his life.

A tall, strapping man wearing black tights and a horizontally striped pull-over turned up, his bike in his hand.

"The Terrible," whispered a little Parisian.

He too had been the recipient of a remarkable name. It was true that he had a hard face with a slight squint, a stout build and used rather direct language, but it was especially when he was turning the pedals that he imposed silence on all the others.

So in this way, the two favorites, the little Maurice and the big Hippolyte were brought together by their extravagant nicknames. But why had they been so resolutely designated as favorites?

Why was everyone so sure that apart from them there was so little chance for anyone else to win? Cycling, already rich after 15 years of racing, now had its bicycle companies. The categories of riders were well established. Recognized professionals, the two favorites had all the required attributes: strength, professionalism and professional equipment. It only remained for them to demonstrate that they were "on form." Moreover, they knew how to train.

However, Garin's record was more impressive than that of Aucouturier. But this was mainly due to their difference in age. There was seven years difference between the two of them. But the age difference could not be seen on their faces.

Garin's strength furnished an irrepressible energy and a flawless endurance. He could ride 200 kilometers without eating and no rider could drop him. With his small size he was able to show remarkable dexterity. Where the others fell or rode over the ruts and punctured, he evaded the dangers and the risks.

He had made his cycling debut ten years earlier in long distance races on the track, which was the main venue for races. He very quickly took his place among the best of them. It was the era when 24-hour races were at the height of their popularity. One day in the winter of 1894 he went down in history. He dominated the specialists such as the Briton Linton and the Breton Corre, a former rival of Terront. He then lined up at the start of a famous eight-day race, inspired by the original six day races where a man was alone on the track for twelve hours a day. This time because it was just eight hours a day, he only finished fifth. It was too short a time for him to show fully his basic strength. He turned seriously to the road in 1896, finishing fourth in Paris-Roubaix. It was a successful apprenticeship, as he triumphed there the following year, outstripping the tough Cordang and Frederick, the same Frederick who was this same day at the Hotel Reveil-Matin, making his return after struggling through a bad period in his career. 1897 again saw Maurice Garin in good form when he nearly defeated the famous Gaston Rivierre in the Bordeaux-Paris, the then "Queen" of the road races.

In 1898, he again went home from the Paris-Roubaix with the winner's bouquet. 1899 was the year of an astonishing Bordeaux-Paris. Pacing by tandems, triplets and motorized bicycles was abandoned in favor of more powerful machines, the motorcars. But as the roads were in a pitiful state, the increased speed was dangerous, all riders crashed several times. Garin only finished third while "The Baker's Boy," Constant Huret, received the laurels. The following year, after the race reverted to a more humane formula, he finished second, behind the German, Joseph Fischer.

He also managed third spot in Paris-Roubaix. There were reasons for believing that he would not win anything else. So when in 1901, Paris-Brest-Paris started, he was not among the favorites. But, he won. In 1902 he returned victoriously from Bordeaux-Paris. Then came 1903 and the Tour de France, where, as we all know, Maurice Garin entered into legend.

And "The Terrible," Hippolyte Aucouturier? The man had not achieved the same glory as his rival. Although he had won a lot of races and some of them very good ones indeed, he was unsuccessful in "The Big Loop" the previous year. Born in Commentry in 1876, he was known for his power, his tenacity and his sprint. He burst onto the scene in 1900 when he finished fifth in Bordeaux-Paris. The following year he took second spot in the same race behind Lesna and was third in the Paris-Brest-Paris won by Garin, when he did not figure among the favorites at the start. 1903 saw him join the ranks of the greats when he triumphed at Roubaix in the race from Paris and again in the capital after arriving first from Bordeaux. He was immediately designated as the number one rival to Garin in the first Tour de France. Unfortunately, a gastric disorder forced his retirement in the very first stage. Disqualified for the overall classification, he took advantage of the rule which permitted him to contest the other stages. And what do you think he did? He treated himself to two victories, one at Marseille and one at Toulouse. But this time it was different. Under the rules of 1904, no rider who had retired on one stage was permitted to start another. So Aucouturier was present at the start of this Tour de France, crowned with the glory of a recent triumph in the Paris-Roubaix.

Several other roadmen, however, deserve mention as starters. There were: Francois Beaugendre from Orleans, Ferdinand Payan from Ales, Chevalier from Moulins, Julien Samson from Brussels, and the Italian Giovanni Gerbi and the Swiss Michel Frederick. The rest of them were mainly there to experience their own personal adventure. A man from the back streets of Paris was busy telling anyone who was prepared to listen, that Cornet was going to surprise quite of few of them. Everyone here knew Henri Cornet. He was from Choisy-le-Roi, a little place just down the road which could be reached by boat along the Seine and was a popular place on high holy days and weekends. So, being so close to Paris, he was the local favorite. He was 20 years-old and had recently left the ranks of the amateurs.

The rules concocted by Desgrange kept the bicycle manufacturer's executives away from the race as much as possible and tended to remove the concept of the team. However, it only prevented the makes of bicycles and tires from being displayed although the riders of the same team were not prepared to disassociate themselves from each other. In this way the riders of La Francaise were the best represented.

They were very dashing these La Francaise riders, Garin's teammates with their black tights and their white jackets. The white jacket was the most notable part of their dress. Underneath they wore a woolen jersey, light or dark, according to their taste. According to the temperature and the controls, they either took the jacket off or left it on. Either way, there was no advertising on any of their clothes.

The jacket, as far as a cycling race was concerned, was a novelty. It was a complete break from the system inherited from horse racing. The very first riders were obliged to wear a jockey's blouse. Then more functional jerseys were accepted, always on the condition that their colors were close to those of the federation. It was in this way that Desgrange, when he raced, had chosen a black jersey with an illusion of white. Generally speaking the riders were less imaginative, normally being content to add just a little bit of color. Terront, for example, could formerly be recognized by a black jersey with a pale blue band.

At the start of this Tour de France, Aucouturier could easily be recognized by his jersey. It was much like the old, traditional ones. He had a liking for a particular pullover, striped red and blue and buttoned at the left shoulder. It would have been necessary for all his jerseys to have been in the wash for him to have changed the style.

The start at Montgeron, on the edge of Villeneuve-Saint-George, had the advantage of being in the country but with easy access to Paris, a mere 15 kilometers away.

The easiest way for the Parisians to reach the spot was by bicycle. While bicycles had been in common use for a good ten years, and the prices had been steadily falling, they were not yet cheap. Especially in these times of economic hardship for most workmen and minor employees. But after saving up, a new bicycle was well within reach. What an advantage after a period not long past when the only individual mount was a horse. Now, there was no more hay to buy. Certainly, a bike still cost 250 francs,[1] which was more than the average monthly salary. But now, they could be purchased second-hand. But you had to be careful and keep it safely stored for theft was on the increase.

The second way of access to Montgeron was by train. Just 19 minutes from the Gare de Lyon by a direct train and an additional half an hour on the bus.

Little by little the area became covered with people. An onlooker had just estimated that there were 4,000 people present. The cries of the newsboys selling *L'Auto* added to the atmosphere. The edition dated the second of July was selling for five centimes. Those selling *Le Velo* were more discreet, as theirs was not the organizing paper. This did not stop the editor from writing about the event, giving the route and the general classification. What's more Charles Ravaud was one of the young columnists. He had just given a friendly wave to Géo Lefèvre.

"Well Géo, how are you? Ready for work? You won't be short of it during this Tour de France!"

"That's true. But I'm not doing badly at *L'Auto*."

"Looking forward to reading you. I notice that you've found your niche. You did well leaving *Le Velo*."

"In fact I didn't leave it. Giffard simply threw me out. He could not put up with me going to *L'Auto* to talk to Victor Goddet. I quickly found myself in the street. The only thing to do to make a living was to go back to Faubourg Monmartre. Fortunately, with Desgrange, everything went well from the start."

Victor Breyer, another well-known journalist, had also just arrived at Villeneuve-Saint-Georges, with the photographers of *La Vie Grand Air,* who promptly took their magnesium flashes into the interior of the cafe already filled with riders and officials.

A trio of riders had just entered the cafe and were immediately the center of attention. They were, Maurice Garin, his brother Cèsar, and Lucien Pothier. They had been offered a glass of coffee and while they were stirring these, a first photographer's flash lit the room. Such was the strength of it that it lit up the straw hats, the caps, but above all it made everybody blink. Although photos were popular, no one appreciated being blinded in the process. Some riders even went so far as to complain to the organizers about the expended magnesium powder. Not only did it blind you, it burnt as well.

So 4,000 spectators and 88 riders were pressing together in this suburb to the south of Paris. There were three categories of riders. The first two comprised the serious racers and they were the "sealed ones," those who could benefit at the controls from help from the bicycle manufacturers who they represented. As for the last group, it was made up of riders who had to race without support. They had been given a rather derogatory title, "The Disinherited." But, in fact, they were not abandoned, always finding the support of a club cyclist, or someone else equally generous but always anonymous. Moreover, they received the solicitude of Georges Abran who was at their disposal at the stage towns. So "Monsieur Abran" was very popular among the ranks of "The Little Ones."

The riders on "sealed machines" were obliged to cover the whole route on the same bike. Their machines were stamped with brass wire and "sealed." Even the hubs of their wheels were treated in the same fashion. This treatment was accepted in a light-hearted manner, and its object was to prove the strength of the bikes and to permit the manufacturers to gain the maximum amount of publicity from it. It was known that one competitor rode several Tours de France using the original seals. If these "Sealed Ones" were more spoiled than the "Disinherited Ones," then they were not part of the upper group who were allowed to borrow a replacement bike, no matter what make of bicycle, in case of mechanical problems.

The bicycles had been sealed in the courtyard of *L'Auto*, over the previous few days, for the majority of the starters. But there were some riders from the provinces whose bikes remained to be done. So this final operation took place just before the start. The few remaining riders had been ordered to present themselves three or four hours before the others.It was in the hotel's courtyard that the operation was completed. One of the staff of *L'Auto* was in charge of the maneuver, helped by four mechanics. Next to them were the tables where the riders signed in and received their numbered armbands.

Jean Dargassies was the first to arrive. He had hurried to make sure that his signature was the first to be on the sheet.

"I've done it!" he declared with his Toulousian accent. "That will bring me good luck!"

Another strapping fellow, Emile Poupin, of Bordeaux, put pen to paper just after. He would like to have preceded Dargassies but he had become lost in Paris, surrounded by handcarts, carriages and motorcars. Stuck in the traffic!

All sorts of celebrities had appeared, some were loquacious and others more tight-lipped.

Later, when the Garins and Pothier arrived, the public came to realize that the race was no longer a dream. The serious part was about to begin. The competitors responded to all the encouragement, they were relaxed and sure of themselves.

In front of the hotel, a small stall had been set up selling hot chocolate, a popular and pleasant drink that was to be found at most outdoor events.

"Come on men, come here!" shouted a photographer to some of the riders. "Have a drink on me. We'll take some photos." Those who were called did not need a second bidding. Dargassies came forward, always ready for a laugh, as well as Maurice Carrère, Alois Catteau and a fourth one whose name no one could remember.

"Keep your bikes," said the man with the black cloth over his huge camera.

"There's no room, it's not practical," replied Catteau.

"You're cyclists, aren't you?" insisted the photographer.

And under the amused gaze of an excited crowd, the four knights posed, holding their steel mounts in one hand and clinking their glasses of chocolate with the other. It was one for the road, the last before the start. They too wore white jackets over dark pullovers. Each of them was entwined by a tubular tire, in case of problems on the road.

Further away, two "disinherited" were engaged in conversation with a rather cheeky Parisian.

"What are you going to get out of all of this?"

They looked at each other, as if the question was rather an ill-chosen one, then one of them replied: "It won't be a fortune! If we're among the first twenty-two finishers we'll get 100F each. In the stages, it's quite different, there are no prizes below eighth place, and we know our limitations."

"Why aren't you tempted to 'mix it' with the stars?"

"For them, it's their job, they're strong, they've all ridden Bordeaux-Paris and Paris-Roubaix. We're just amusing ourselves.

We don't race at all. It is only because we know how to ride 300 kilometers in a day and we are better than most cyclists in our area that we're champions. We're going to do our best, that's all."

"So it's going to cost you money?" the Parisian continued.

"Perhaps not. We're going for some of the 'primes' on the road. They're giving fifty of them at five francs a day. You need to ride at more than 12 kilometers an hour. Even we can do that."

So everyone could take part in the Tour de France. All that was needed was to sign in and hang on.

A newsboy for *L'Auto* split up the group which had formed around the "Disinherited" and the cheeky Parisian. He continued to shout his blurb, "Everything on the Tour de France! The starters, the stages, the prizes!"

Someone's curiosity was aroused: "Give me one, I want to see how much the stars are going to get."

Everything was printed and out in the open.

First Stage, Paris-Lyon. For the winner and the placed riders: 750, 350, 175, 100, 50, 25 Francs.

Second stage: Lyon-Marseille: 500 Francs for the winner and prizes down to seventh place.

Third Stage, Marseille-Toulouse: 400 Francs for the winner and prizes down to seventh place.

Fourth Stage, Toulouse-Bordeaux: 350 Francs for the winner and prizes down to seventh place.

Fifth Stage, Bordeaux-Nantes: 600 Francs for the winner and prizes down to seventh place.

Sixth Stage, Nantes-Paris, Merged with the general classification which is: 1st: 5,000F; 2nd: 3,000F; 3rd: 1,500F; 4th: 1,000F; 5th: 500F; 6th: 400F; 7th: 300F; 8th: 200F; 9th - 22nd: 100F.

It turned out that the first to finish were paid like real professionals, especially for the general classification. This compared favorably with other events. In this same year, the winner of Paris-Roubaix had received 1,000F and the next victor in the Bol d'Or would take home 3,000F. This latter race was lucrative because it took place on a track which was filled to the brim with paying spectators. The Buffalo Velodrome, which had welcomed the race for many years, vibrated to the rhythm of its 24 heroic hours. But, road or track, these were long distance races and, in fact, their winners earned only peanuts in comparison with the princes of the arenas, the sprinters.

As strange as may seem, 1904 was not among the most lucrative years for the cycling industry. Certainly bicycles were still selling well and profit margins were respectable for the manufacturers of accessories as well as for the assemblers of complete machines. But they no longer constituted the pivot of their commercial strategy. A number of them had branched out and were now making motorcars. And the press had jumped on the bandwagon. It has already been noted that the wealthy classes had almost totally abandoned the bicycle. Gone was the period when it was common for a king, an aristocrat or a wealthy celebrity to be seen on a bicycle. Incidentally this snobbish aspect invaded the pages of the journals for only a few years, but they were, from 1892 to 1898, unequalled jewels of aestheticism. In 1904, the world of the rich once again demonstrated its passion for the horse or expressed itself with the dashing horse-power of the automobile, which was becoming ever more sensational.

There remained only the owner of a steel horse to be interested in cycling races. That was why there were no expensive carriages, motorized or harnessed, to be seen at Montgeron on this Saturday, the second of July. That the Tour de France is a sociological phenomenon was plain for all to see.

The riders, these champions from deepest France, became the heralds of the most unknown villages as they always had their heroes. It was in this way that Jean Dargassies, a pleasant man, became known as "The Blacksmith of Grisolles," that Lucien Pothier appeared as "The Butcher of Sens," and that Jean-Baptiste Dortignacq, the man from Peyrehorade, was "The Landais Dortignacq."

A large number of spectators were inspecting the competitor's bikes, some of which were simply leaning unguarded against the walls and the fence around the hotel. Others were stacked together in pairs, rather like shocks of corn. While the riders talked with each other, occasionally an onlooker would touch the tools of their trade. A young man in a straw hat put his hands on the saddle and the handlebars of a bike.

"Careful," a roadman in a white jacket growled at him.

"I only wanted to feel the weight, monsieur," replied the boy, somewhat intimidated.

"Don't worry, it's eleven and a half kilos, just like Garin's. It's a champion's bike.

Other interested spectators gathered round and entered into a discussion. It was like a circle of technicians who verbally dismantled the bikes.

They were particularly struck by Aucouturier's machine. It was a Peugeot, which was no doubt why he was doing better that year. But the choice of equipment hardly differed from one rider to another. One thing they all had in common was that there were no gears. These were left to the tourists. Desgrange played a major role here as he did not believe the principle of variable gears worthy of true racers. Here, the chain was of the double-roller, inch-pitch type. A spectator revealed that Aucouturier had chosen 24 x 9, being a gear of 5.85 meters. Even if this inquisitive onlooker had made a mistake when counting the teeth, he could not have been far from the truth. On the road it was rare to use anything bigger, as it was not worth climbing the hills on foot. Aucouturier this time was using a freewheel. The principle had proved its worth, offering a new advantage as you no longer had to pedal on the descent. Like most top riders, "The Terrible" had chosen tubular tires which were already known as "tubs." Thirty millimeters in diameter, they were glued to wooden rims. But other riders were happy with wired-on tires on either wood or aluminum rims. Like that of Garin, his bike was appropriately enamelled black on an overcast day.

"What types of cranks has he got?" asked someone.

"170 millimeters. Now, there's a choice of from 155 to 175," replied a middle-aged man with a cap on.

"Have you seen his spokes? They're reinforced at both ends."

"That's important, if you don't want to break too many of them!"

Nobody asked questions about the handlebars as everyone knew what they were like. That year the most popular ones were "like those of the police," wide and not too curved. But when the bikes were being inspected and sealed, it was noticed that some of them were equipped with handlebars which allowed three different positions for the hands. For accessories most of these valiant roadmen had a little bag attached to the handlebars where they carried a wrench, perhaps a spoke key, while also leaving room for a hat or a scarf. Many of them carried a little money. They needed it for possible expenses on the road and in the stage towns.

For the two hours that he had been in the vicinity of the Hotel

Reveil-Matin, Abran had been relaxed and spent the time conversing with various people. When he arrived things were quite calm and peaceful. He greeted the owner of the bistro, who had promptly offered him his favorite drink. What do you expect, it was after seven in the evening! Just because it was a serious occasion did not mean that you had to break all your habits, did it? Abran saw the crowd arrive.

He was now surrounded by the crowd as he consulted his watch. The countdown had begun. He hurried to call the riders. A man in a white jacket was very agitated. The crowd pressed around him.

"My bike's been stolen! I left it in front of a cafe at Villeneuve!"

A spectator looked at his armband — number 101. It was Serres, a rider from Rochefort. How unfortunate! And he had 150F in the bag on his handlebars. All his savings!

Serres would not be starting. Abran was unable to do anything for him. It was 8:45 p.m. The control was closed.

"Gentlemen! To the starting line!"

On the road and on the pavement there was an indescribable crush. The riders had to fight their way through. The starting line was 500 meters away and marked by a big banner across the road. Georges Abran, in a loud voice called the men, one by one. One of them did not reply. It was Serres, for him the event had become a tragedy.

While Abran was expected to release the field immediately, here he was giving a clear speech.

"Gentlemen, I think it would be useful to remind you of some of the essential points of the rules. Would you be good enough to give me your attention for a few moments."

And Abran went on to emphasize that all organized help on the road was prohibited. Although no pacers were permitted that did not mean a passing cyclist was unable to approach them. They were allowed to receive food from such a stranger and perhaps even borrow a bike from him. He also reminded them that all these details were very clearly laid out in the rules and that everyone should have studied them closely. An engine started up, it was the Cotterreau automobile belonging to *L'Auto*. The vehicle disappeared from view. Total silence ensued. Abran picked up his flag. In his other hand he gripped his pistol.

"Attention gentlemen!" he cried.

The revolver shot rang out. It was 9 o'clock in the evening. Night was beginning to fall.

---

1 If you multiply by eight you would have a realistic equivalent of french francs of today.

Chapter 3
Paris-Lyon

Objective: Lyon, at the end of 467 kilometers of dusty roads, ruts and badly cobbled towns. The previous year's route had been retained, through Fontainbleau, Montgargis, Cosne, Nevers, Moulins, Roanne and Tarare. The 1903 experience proved that the best of them would take eighteen hours to reach the town of silk manufacturers. It was in order that the stage would finish on Sunday afternoon - for the benefit of the spectators - that the start had been fixed for 9 o'clock on Saturday evening.

The organization had progressed in the Cotterreau, the motor-car which was to follow the competitors from start to finish. Géo Lefèvre would no longer have to take the train nor resort to his bicycle. Except for a mechanical breakdown he would arrive at the same time as the riders. And above all he would be able to "watch" some of them very closely. It was said that some of them were inclined to cheat, especially during the night. The "three-cylinder Cotterreau" should prove to be useful. Géo Lefèvre had been given an assistant, Jean Miral, a man who if he knew little about cycling and its mysteries, was keen to learn. There was, of course, a chauffeur, the "bold" Ouzou, an expert in the field as he was the owner of a large garage in Paris.

For the moment, only Miral was being driven by Ouzou. Lefèvre had gone on in front to organize the secret control. None of the others knew where it would be. Henri Desgrange had delegated his executive powers to him. The young journalist had already said straight out that, "We will disqualify without pity all the competitors caught cheating or who have broken the rules concerning pacers or helpers." But he had no police experience and just hoped that all would be well. The means of controlling the race was not limited to a single car. There was also a motorcyclist as assistant commissioner. His principle duty was to precede the racers and to shuttle between the groups of riders. It was revealed that his motorcycle was the last word in mechanical ingenuity as it was supplied with a gear change. Furthermore, its driver was no ordinary man, he was Gaston Rivierre, the triple winner of Brodeaux-Paris and, just three years ago, second to Maurice Garin in Paris-Brest-Paris. *L'Auto* knew how to use the name of a champion to draw the people in!

The duties of the organizers were obviously not the same as those of the riders. Ready to assume theirs, the cyclists took off at top speed. Was this possible over such a distance? The best of them were already at the front, Aucouturier, Garin and Frederick. They were pulling the peloton along. But the peloton did not comprise 87 riders, the 87 riders who had answered the call of Monsieur Abran. In fact its number had doubled since leaving Paris. The organizers did not wish to stop anonymous cyclists from mixing in with the champions. And would they have been able to do so anyway? The journalist Francois Mercier had started with the stars. He would be able to give his impressions of the first few kilometers to the readers of *L'Auto*.

The pace was very fast. The pedalers who had started before the professionals were rapidly caught. Not all of them were skillful on a bike. Aucouturier had already had to scream at some of them who were not keeping their bikes straight. These "pedards"[1] believed themselves to be as good as the rest but, in reality, many of them were quite dangerous.

Dangerous? Crashes, several of them bit the dust! The air was blue. Ten men were on the ground. Including some of the best, those who had been riding at the front. Bikes tangled together. There were: Pothier, Beaugendre, Gerbi, Lapre, Hibon, Blanqui, Daumain, Lipman and... Aucouturier. Garin, skillful as always and careful as never before, avoided the crash. Some of them were immediately back on their bikes and embarked on a vigorous chase.

Garin turned to his brother who was sharing in this adventure and shouted, "Go, Cèsar! It's not the time to think about it."

"What about Pothier, Maurice?"

"Just go, we'll see about him later."

And the two men increased the pace which had already been fast. Here they were at Corbeil, twenty-seven minutes after they had left Villeneuve-Saint-Georges, having covered eighteen kilometers. A fine performance, as it was dark and the road was not wonderful. A cry was heard at the back. It was Pothier. He had already rejoined the leading group, with Lambeuf, another victim of the crash. Further behind it was noticed that one man was still missing. Alas it was Aucouturier.

"We've got to go hard," said the eldest of the Garins, again.

In the illuminated passage through Corbeil, the spectators were dumbfounded. They had the impression of seeing the demons announced by Desgrange passing through. What speed they were doing on their apocalyptic machines. Someone remarked that Aucouturier in his striped blue and red jersey had not come through. Here he was at last, more than five minutes down. Here, they knew nothing about the crash. No one knew that Lipman had broken his bicycle and fractured the index finger of his left hand. They knew nothing of Adrien Blanqui's misfortune, another unlucky acrobat. They did not know that he had been unable to find his bike when he recovered from his crash. He was perplexed. Had it been stolen? He had shouted into the night, but no one could tell him what had happened to his beautiful machine. He still hoped - in his handlebar bag, there was his license, with his name of course.

During this time the leading group were going very hard. Here was Melun already, the 35th kilometer. One hour and one minute on the road. Real racers, these men! Suddenly a profusion of light; it was a control. An official one. The crowd presses around. There is no lack of color, with a great number of army officers appearing from the neighboring garrison. A rider shouts out his number: No. 1. It is Garin. It is only natural at this point in the race, but he is far from being the only one. There is a scramble to record the numbers of the others. Later it is revealed that Chevalier is already 14 minutes down.

Fontainbleau is just as welcoming. All of those present have their hearts seized with emotion. There too, the officers have come to take part in the spectacle. Clamour and applause greet the passage of Garin and his accompanists. The first 53 kilometers have been covered in one hour and 30 minutes. Pothier is at the back, handicapped by a bicycle damaged in the crash. As for Aucouturier, he arrives only ten minutes after the leaders. Chevalier is clocked in half an hour down.

Nemours. A town just like any other on the route. No control here. But what is happening? Mounted policemen are barring the way. One of the leaders cannot avoid them and falls beneath the horses' hooves. The others barely succeed in stopping. The cops hurl insults. The rider who fell is the recipient of the worst of the abuse. Unfortunately, all these horsemen had wanted to do was to help them avoid a dangerous section of the road. The cyclists restart, under the eyes of a band of enthusiasts who would very much like to have taken the side of these gallant roadmen but who feared the forces of law and order.

Montargis, at the 102nd kilometer marker. Some sort of picture of the race could be established thanks to the flying control. Here the riders were permitted to take on food and even change their machines. No worries for the elder Garin whose white jacket is the figurehead. The time was recorded as being 23 minutes past midnight and Garin was accompanied by about 20 others. The average speed was more than 30 kph, in spite of the dark and the pitfalls and traps. On the other hand, things were not going well for Pothier whose deficit was fifteen minutes. He changed his bike with its buckled wheels for one in better order and restarted immediately. But this was a long time before Aucouturier, who arrived covered in blood and was complaining of more crashes. "The Terrible" was now 43 minutes down on Maurce Garin. But there was no question of him retiring. He was thinking of the following stages.

The night was very black, favorable to fantasies... and cheating. But this was expected, hence the infamous secret control. It was at Briare that those in power had established the next one. It was set up a few kilometers before the town. Impossible to avoid it! And especially not to see it as an enormous banner was employed, lit up by headlights. A complete encampment had been set up with tables and chairs. A large number of the townspeople were there, as the occasion was worth staying up for.

An illuminated signal had been placed 200 meters before the mandatory stop. No rider could say that he had not had sufficient warning. Géo Lefèvre, the organizer of and attentive witness to the operation used his pen to describe the scene. "Two kilometers before the town, in the middle of the fields, we installed the secret control where all the riders were obliged to get off their bikes and give a signature. This lonely spot this evening presented a curious spectacle. The road was encircled by lanterns which pierced the darkness of the night sky with their luminous globes. Cut-out signs using huge letters displayed the words: 'HALT! CONTROL'. And under the acetylene lamp, in front of a table were waiting, like me, the controllers and a crowd of villagers, cyclists and drivers who had all organized a small but picturesque campsite.

"A luminous trail came towards us, two dusty drivers called me over. It was Ouzou and Miral, with whom I had to rush down to Lyon. Quickly, the news. 'There's a dozen in front, going like madmen. Pothier was dropped after a puncture. Aucouturier seems already to be out of the running, he has fallen three times and is now 45 minutes down.'

"And there on the horizon the agreed-upon signal has been lit. A green Bengal lantern, and then when it was still throwing its pallid light, a thick cloud came towards us and, in the middle of this cloud, there were bodies, shiny steel, legs wildly turning. A cry was heard, 'STOP! CONTROL!'"

The register was open. At 11:15 p.m. Maurice Garin signed in, in company with twelve other riders and with... Chevalier. Was this possible? He had been reported to have been dropped as much at Melun as at Fontainbleau where his deficit was 30 minutes.

Several riders relieved themselves while Cèsar Garin was the first away. This man was no second-rate rider. Certainly, he could not hope to rival his elder brother. But his recently acquired record already included some very respectable places. In this year of 1904, in the process of training for the Tour, he finished second in Paris-Roubaix, only half a length down on Aucouturier who won with an average speed of 33.5 kph; then he took third spot in Bordeaux-Paris behind Georget and Petit-Breton, both absent from this Tour de France.

Where are the others, the Pothiers and the Aucouturiers? Pothier arrives at last. He has already made up a few minutes and is now only 12 minutes behind. Had he increased his pace or did the Garin group ease off a bit? There is no way of knowing. As for "The Terrible," he is, as they say "nowhere to be seen." To complete the picture, if Pothier went through 12 minutes after the leaders, he was preceded by seven minutes by riders like Maitron, Payan and Cornet who we will be able to use as reference points.

At Cosne, although no official control had been set up, a dining hall had been opened. It was very profitable for the owner of the Tivoli Cafe, whose establishment was invaded by more than 500 customers. But this place was also to the benefit of several obervers: certain peculiarities were in evidence. If the Garin brothers, Beaugendre, Frederick, Gerbi, Antoine Faure and some others were seen together, like they were at Briare, Pothier had now rejoined them. Twelve minutes gained in 31 kilometers! The troubling thing was that Payan and Cornet who had been 7 minutes in front of him at Briare now went through 18 minutes behind him. Which constitutes a "differential" of 25 minutes! And that is by no means all. Julieu Maitron, who was in the company of the two riders had lost even more. Pothier had taken 32 minutes out of him! Did all these riders suffer from punctures and did Pothier prove to be better than the leading group? An explanation was needed!

En route for the fixed control at Nevers, where they were resolutely waiting for the riders. Three local cycling clubs had offered their services and some motorcyclists had agreed to "cover" the route, from Cosne to Moulins. At the first glimmer of daylight, seven other sporting societies, from Morvan to Berry, had reinforced them, with the object of supporting them. Above the control, a banner had been put up. It read, "Hommage to the young stars of Nievre and to their compatriots of the Tour de France, Chevalier and Maitron." It is the latter who is of interest to us at the moment. Wait for him to arrive, then we will be more sure of his time deficit.

For the moment, here is the Cotterreau motorcar. It announces the arrival of the leaders. On offer is water, coffee, soup and fruits. Here they are, at 4:55 a.m. There are seven of them: Maurice Garin, Pothier, Jousselin, Frederick, Chevalier, Jeack and Gerbi. Some are happy just to take water. Garin takes his favorite, soup, while Pothier shouts, "A bicycle! Give me a bicycle to fit me!"

Everything is ready. He gets one. His face lights up into a smile. And the group leaves as it arrived, at top speed.

Scarcely five minutes go by and the second group appears, with Cèsar Garin, Beaugendre, Gauban, Pillon, Roggisnoli,

Lombard and Laeser. The masseurs remain with their arms at their sides, as the group leaves as soon as possible.

At 5:05 a.m. Faure, the man from St. Etienne arrives. With good intentions he approachs the control sheet to sign it. The paper was already dirty. You should see the state of the riders' hands!

Cheers rang out. They could only be addressed to a Nivernais. It was Maitron, who quickly indicated that he had punctured, so he was slightly distanced from the front group. Pothier's return to the front group was without any such explanation.

They were beginning to worry about Aucouturier. Just before 6 o'clock, they saw him arrive, his face swollen and one of his wrists sprained. He was applauded for his courage and his valor. He had made up his mind to stop and receive treatment for his injuries. It gave him the chance to talk about his problems to those who wanted to listen.

"You can call me clumsy, but I don't think I was. At the start, Garin, Frederick and myself were occupying the width of the road, as we had decided to let no one past. Several adversaries and several intruding cyclists edged their way past on the verge, cut in front and then fell. Garin got past, I saw the road was clear and went past too, when a 'twit' ran into the side of me and knocked me down! Was that my fault? The incident cost me 15 minutes. At Nemours, I punctured! No spare tire, I rode on the rim, when Samson went past and agreed to lend me a tubular which he helped me to fit. More time lost."

"You had no spare tire?" asked a spectator who continued, "What about your spare tire?"

"No, fortunately Samson was there to pass me one."

No one dared to question "The Terrible" further on this lack of foresight. Furthermore everyone was pleased that no rider fell on the descent of Pougues-les-Eaux situated 12 kilometers before Nevers. Its length and tight bends had trapped many before. There was a warning sign financed by De Dion-Bouton (an automobile company), but many thought that the local clubs should have installed a first-aid post there was well.

Suddenly two riders arrived riding in the opposite direction to the race. They were Jaeck and Laeser. Jaeck had been in the front group. What had happened to him? He had fallen and injured himself. For him it was a catastrophe. He was going to return to Paris with his friend Laeser.

Someone remarked that Nevers was the half-way point in the stage. So the hardest part remained to be done. Now that the sun was risen, people started to wonder what weather the riders were going to meet. For several days the whole of France had been enduring very hot weather indeed. So much so that women had been using their parasols. Today, it might still be just as hot.

The second fixed control was organized at Moulins, after the riders had covered 281 kilometers. Since Nevers, the front group had been riding in daylight. They were on the Route Nationale No. 7. They were not bothered by traffic. There were very few vehicles in the area. On these roads the principle form of transport ran on hay, the horse. Many of them were harnessed, pulling carts and other farm vehicles. Herds of cows often filled the roads as well. One group of them even delayed the riders. They had to wait for them to cross the road. "Charolais," said Chevalier, a local man who knew his cattle well. The countryside smelled good. There were large golden sheaves of wheat. Just before Moulins, a peal of bells rang out from a village.

"The Angelus!" Garin remarked.

His companion Pothier did not say a word. He was too busy pedaling.

Moulins. 6:53 a.m. "And 24 seconds," said the timekeeper to his neighbor who was recording the times. Here, they needed to be precise. Once again, the area around the control was thick with people. The applause broke out for Maurcie Garin, Chevalier, Frederick, Pillon, Gerbi and Pothier who had all just signed in. They drank and took some food. Garin greedily swallowed his soup. The Cotterreau arrived just after. They had to wait for a quarter of an hour for the signatures of Garin junior, Jousselin, Beaugendre, Gauban and Lombard who did not hang around longer than necessary either. Three quarters of an hour behind the leaders were Payan and Faure, followed by Maitron. Aucouturier did not arrive before 8:37. A huge deficit: 1 hour 40 minutes. And still 186 kilometers to go!

This time "The Terrible" seemed depressed. There was a pathetic expression on his bloody face.

"Alibert! Go and find Alibert for me!" he shouted.

His manager arrived with a wet sponge. He ran it over his face.

"Do you want something to eat?" Alibert asked.

"I'm cooked. Give me something to drink, chocolate, or

milk."

Did they know what he was going to ask for? A bowl was already steaming next to him. It was held out to him and Aucouturier drank slowly. He was short of breath. People were struck by the redness of his eyes, affected by the darkness and the dust on the road.

At last he restarted.

The next fixed control was at Roanne, 100 kilometers further on. It was quite a distance. They had gone past the mines at Moulins. In the front group some were fresher than others. Certainly something was going to happen. Garin seemed quite frisky.

Perhaps this was the hill of Varenne-sur-Allier. Garin was not sure. Even so he said to Pothier, "Hold on, this time we're going."

The "Butcher of Sens" still felt strong. He did not flinch when "The Little Chimney Sweep" attacked on the hill. He was even seen to do his turn at the front. The group exploded. Pillon, a young man, had been struggling for some time was left behind. Chevalier and Beaugendre pedaled at the same pace. Only Gerbi and Frederick - real riders these - tried to resist.

Another hill, an even steeper one, presented itself. Gerbi who only knew a few words of French, managed to make himself understood when he suggested climbing it on foot. This sort of thing never surprised a roadman. Their single gear was often a crippling disadvantage on the steeper gradients.

Scarcely had Frederick agreed to this than Garin attacked strongly again. Pothier jumped on his wheel and followed easily. Gerbi tried to hang on as Frederick gave up the struggle. It only remained for the two Frenchmen to unite their efforts to open a gap. Garin could have dropped Pothier. But he was a teammate. And time passed more quickly when there were two of you. Once again, the wind had come up and was holding them back. The two riders were working together.

The Cotterreau automobile was never very far from them. Garin made a sign to the driver and drew closer to the car. Lefèvre observed the maneuver. He felt the champion wanted to speak to him.

"Géo!" Garin called.

"What do you want, Maurice?"

"What have you got to eat in the car?"

"Some chicken and some bread. You..." Surprised, Lefèvre hesitated. But not for long. He replied, "Even so, you don't want to..."

Garin interrupted him. "Yes! Give me the chicken and the bread. I've nothing left to eat. As you know it's 100 kilometers from Moulins to Roanne."

"Maurice, you're mad! What about the rules!"

"I don't care about your rules. Pothier and I are hungry, that's all."

"It's impossible."

"Do you want me to pack it in?"

"You'll be all right. I know you, Maurice. Just ease off a bit."

"I said give me your chicken, Géo."

The young Lefèvre was petrified. What a situation! They spoke of leaving the race! They had already lost Aucouturier. If Garin retired it would be a catastrophe. And he did not look as if he was joking.

Suddenly Garin stopped pedaling. Ouzou drove the Cotterreau into a field.

"You wouldn't do that to me?" asked the journalist.

"Not if you give me something to eat!"

The dialogue went no further, Géo Lefèvre was already putting his hand into the basket. He fed the two team mates. Miral did not say a word. His mouth already full, Garin tried to conclude the conversation in his own way.

"...and remember that there is no shame in giving someone something to eat."

"That you should make a moral code take precedence over a rule of circumstance, is beyond question!" Géo Lefèvre said to himself.

Just before Roanne, at the top of a hill, Garin turned around and saw a cloud of dust in the distance. It was another cyclist.

"Chevalier is not far behind," he said to Pothier. "It's incredible! Where has he come from? He's a strange man, this Chevalier. He always gives the impression of not going very well, he's always being dropped, but at the controls he's never very far behind us."

A strange sense of happiness was being radiated from the Cafe du Bosquet at Roanne. The terrace was flooded in sunlight. There were a few extra tables. Some were occupied by the managers and team assistants. It smelled, at the same time, of rubber tires, massage oils and of good soup. This broth was tasted before being handed to the stars. The other tables were occupied by more formally dressed people. They were involved with the paperwork concerning the race. Those with the registers which were to receive the signatures of the pedalers and those with dispatches to send to their newspapers. They were beginning to pile up as they had been arriving in great numbers. The news was out about everything that had happened between Paris and Moulins. Those who had come from Commentry had long faces as they were supporters of "The Terrible," their fellow citizen. They had been torn between going to Moulins or Roanne before taking the road to the southeast (Roanne). Other Bourbonnais had chosen Moulins. So they were the first to learn of the painful news of the troubles of their rider.

Nobody knew exactly why the cafe was so welcoming but the proprietor had done things well. They were echanging pleasantries while they waited for the arrival of the riders.

Suddenly, they began to sit up and take notice. Dust in the distance. The riders? Here were two of them, Garin and Pothier. They signed in. It is noted that they are not even trembling. What freshness! 10:40 a.m. is inscribed opposite their names. They each swallow a bowl of soup and leave with some food. Chevalier has just arrived, he is only three minutes down on the two La Francaise men. He does not look strong.

What about the others? The tension mounts as the time passes. Two other riders present themselves, filthy and trickling with sweat - Gerbi and Frederick. The Italian signs in while the Swiss fills his stomach. It is this that explains the difference: one clocks in at 11:01 a.m.; the other at 11:03 a.m. They then have to wait a while for a quartet to arrive. They are Cèsar Garin, Lombard, Gauban and Beaugendre. So the younger Garin has already lost three quarters of an hour on his brother.

For the record, the following arrivals were recorded: Jousselin, 12:09; Payan, Cornet, Gabory, 12:21; Aucouturier, Pillon, 12:44; Maitron, 13:01; Dortignacq, Ventresque, 13:17: Noel Prèvost, 13:26; Dargassies, Geay, Durant, 13:33. And the others far, far behind.

Pillon and Maitron had cracked. A dejected Aucouturier was managing his distress as well as he could. He had to hang on until Lyon. After that, it remained to be seen.

Tarare was only 43 kilometers from Roanne. There was, however, a check there. It was to help verify how the race was progressing. The scenery had changed considerably. To the wind which seriously hampered the riders' progress, was now added the hills. Already on the Moulins-Roanne section they had made their appearance, notably between Lapalisse and La Pacaudiere. Although Garin and Pothier had crossed them on their bikes, most of the riders had been obliged to put their feet to the ground. Maitron and Dargassies had done some of this, without speaking of Maisonneuve and of Gauthier who wore out their shoes a little.

It should be made clear that this 1904 Tour de France contained some relics from the past which were destined to continue for quite some time. The gear change existed but was not used. Indeed, it was forbidden. So instead of "polymultiplication," one changed bikes. But only when it was absolutely necessary. That was authorized. Only those with "sealed" machines did not have the right to do so. Here, between Roanne and Tarare where the road often went up, the leaders climbed the hills on their standard bikes. Slowly and with difficulty, but they did manage it.

Garin and Pothier arrived sweating at the Pin Bouchain hill. They had taken off their white jackets at Moulins but had kept their black tights on. You could at least say that this part of their clothing was still in its original color.

The descent to Tarare demanded great skill, as it was as twisty as anyone could want. It was very fortunate that it did not have to be negotiated at night. The two riders started to fly over the potholes at full speed. They were both fully expecting a puncture. Once, Garin, who was leading, went right into the middle of a pile of sand, just imagine how quickly that stopped him.

At last they crossed through Tarare to loud applause. It was just after 12:30. Chevalier arrived at 1:00 p.m. Frederick had dropped Gerbi. It was noted that the time was 1:10; his Italian accomplice arrived only a quarter of an hour later. The quartet led by Cèsar Garin were working perfectly together and were checked in ten minutes later. The others came through one by one. Only Aucouturier and Pillon were together and arrived at three in the afternoon.

A complaint had just arrived. It concerned one of the leading riders. The race organization had been informed. The affair was to be settled later.

For the moment it remained to complete the final 43 kilometers. Garin and Pothier got on with it. Always within striking distance of them were the men of *L'Auto*, in the Cotterreau automobile of Ouzou and Rivierre's motorbike. This time the car was in front.

Rivierre was talking to the two leaders, "Soon over, men?"

"That's true, Gaston, but we're very hungry," Pothier replied. "Would you go to the car and see if there's any chicken left?"

As the triple winner of Bordeaux-Paris did not seem inclined to reply, Garin intervened, "You don't have to think about it. You saw that car just now? They offered us something to eat. We refused. And do you know what the driver said? That he filled his trunk for the riders and that he had already fed a dozen of them behind."

The famous Rivierre, the rider whose beard was even better known than that of Abran, had certainly seen the car. Everything had been perfectly in order. For him Pothier's request, backed up by Garin did not really put him to any inconvenience. Was it not understood that those people in the world of bikes should always help each other out? As he accelerated even with the car, the metal of his machine shone in the sunlight. Was it Miral who passed the remainder of the chicken? Later neither one nor the other could remember!

It only remained for the "Butcher of Sens" to sink his teeth into the bird. It was almost as fresh as when it left Paris. Garin himself, had asked for nothing, he would eat at Lyon and that was an end to it.

The town of Saint-Symphorien-de-Lay had just been passed. A car caught up with the two leaders. Two men were shaking their fists. The vehicle stopped, turned round and drove back to the cyclists. The passengers were visibly agitated. They confronted Garin and Pothier, "We've had enough of your tricks! We're going to make you pay for them. You won't get through Saint-Etienne, we'll get you thrown out. And if you continue, we'll kill you."

Was that all? The local people, lining the side of the road heard everything. They were totally taken aback. The car had a Saint-Etienne number plate. It contained four passengers and was accompanied by a motorbike.

Garin, who did not want to leave things at that, quickly replied, "Leave us alone. Our job is to ride a bike and that's what we're doing."

"Faure is just as good as you. But he hasn't got the same advantages, he's not in on the racket."

"There is no racket. Faure's a good rider, but he's behind, that's all."

"You'll remember at Saint-Etienne, you band of s...!"

Insult was added to threat. Then abruptly he car drove off. Pothier looked at Garin. He was as white as a sheet.

The winner of last year's Tour started pedaling again in earnest, without saying anything. Calm returned and blood was no longer boiling. "The sooner we get this stage over, the better!" Garin thought.

Do you know the Half-Moon? It is a suburb of Lyon, just behind Tessin, the logical extension of the Route Nationale No. 7 coming from Tarare but also from Paris. The stage was to be decided at Les Delices, a large, pleasant open-air cafe. But the locals thought this restaurant to be insufficient and so temporary stands had been erected to welcome the public.

It was overflowing with women and children. The public had been kept completely up to date on the events as only a week before they had talked about a finish at the velodrome. But everything had changed. Here, things were not being run by *L'Auto*. Certainly they had a correspondent here, but it was the Cycling Federation of Lyon who were really organizing things. It was they who had built the stands.

Red, white and blue flags had been attached to the trees and as there were not enough of these, they had erected dozens of posts, five or six meters high in order to display the French colors. On each side of the road near where they thought the finishing line would be, two posts seemed to go all the way up to the sky. Between them had been installed the yellow banner of *L'Auto*. The wind filled it, like a sail, which did not prevent anyone from reading, in the center of it: "Tour de France de *L'Auto*. Arrival Control." And laterally, in the form of an oval, on the left: "Cafe-Restaurant Les Delices" and on the right: "Organized by the FCLSE." Everyone was in on the act!

But this happy and successful cooperation was not to the taste of the U.V.F. The French cycling federation wanted to be omnipotent. Such meddling in its domain did not suit it. It had made the position clear to Desgrange. Had the organizer's license not been granted on the understanding that its rules would be respected?

The restaurant had been extended by a huge marquee with a festooned roof. But the officials had not set up shop here. They had been installed on the other side of the road behind a large wooden panel where the riders were obliged to present themselves.

At the beginning of the afternoon, the area was roasting under a scorching sun. The Lyon crowds had deserted the banks of the river Saone and the river Rhone to crowd here. A road construction company had left piles of large cobblestones, and the pavement was cluttered with them. Women were using them as seats. One of them was daydreaming in the sun, while another, taking advantage of some shade, was looking after a little girl. But the first of these two women was not overcome with the sun as she was holding a parasol above her head. There was no shortage of female spectators, delightfully dressed in their Sunday best. Their long dresses sweeping the ground while their hats defied the muses of creation. The men, more numerous, were done up like princes. With caps for those who had come by bicycle and straw hats for the others. The colors of the cloth bands interlaced with the straw of the hats and competed with the other colors present. Everyone wore a very smart tie. Even if they were hot. It was noticed that no cyclist laid his bike down. They were all carefully kept at hand.

The regional press had organized a formidable publicity campaign for this finish. And as they all now needed to get the full story, representatives of *Le Progres*, of *Lyon Sport*, of *Le Monde Lyonnais,* of *Le Rappel* and of *L'Express*, jostled together.

The Cotterreau had just arrived. Géo Lefèvre had found Monsieur Abran. Both of them were thanking the organizers who, over the previous eight days, had devoted all their efforts into this stage finish. Abran's needs were becoming apparent. For this reason he found solace in the refreshment room.

Géo Lefèvre indicated that the two leaders would not be arriving alone. That is not to say that Chevalier had managed to rejoin them. No, it was the local unknown cyclists who were keeping company with the day's heroes. It was not totally desirable, with their untimely accelerations they were modifying the natural pace of the two champions. They even managed to get in between them. In this way a gap opened in the last kilometer. This was to Garin's advantage who with his usual skill, was able to thread his way through these nuisances who were coming from everywhere.

Chevalier crossed the line only twenty minutes behind the two men. It was a very big surprise. The signs of exhaustion on his face were clear for all to see. Garin, himself had exploded with joy. At the start of the stage he had said that he had no idea of how things were going to work out, what with riders like Aucouturier, Frederick and especially Gerbi, who was very ambitious. Pothier too, was far from being glum; to finish with Garin confirmed his hopes that he would be able to do well. He recalled that before Nevers he was ten minutes down on Garin and that getting back up to him was more than he could have hoped for.

The others arrived, one by one. Were any of them more unlucky than Aucouturier? "The Terrible" refused to say anything. The procession continued all night. Fifty-five riders were classified. The last of them had taken twice as long as Garin to cover the course! It was learned that Jaeck, victim of a serious crash after being in front at Nevers and having turned around to return to Paris, had changed his mind and retaken the road to Lyon. He finished near the back of the field, having demonstrated an extraordinary determination.

But perhaps at this point you would appreciate a break in the tale in order to consult the classification of the first twenty-five.

Stage 1 - Paris - Lyon Results:

1.	Garin, Maurice .... Bicycle La Francaise Tires Dunlop	17h 7 mins 7 secs
2.	Pothier	17h 7 mins 30 secs
3.	Chevalier	17h 27 mins
4.	Frederick	17h 45 mins
5.	Gerbi	17h 50 mins
6.	Garin, Cèsar	18h 12 mins
7.	Beaugendre	18h 12 mins
8.	Lombard	18h 12 mins
9.	Gauban	18h 13 mins
10.	Faure	19h 10 mins
11.	Payan	19h 10 mins
12.	Gabory	19h 32 mins
13.	Cornet	19h 37 mins

14.	Aucouturier	19h	37 mins
15.	Pillon	19h	37 mins
16.	Jousselin	19h	39 mins
17.	Maitron	20h	16 mins
18.	Dortignacq	20h	29 mins
19.	Ventresque	20h	29 mins
20.	Dargassies	21h	4 mins
21.	Prèvost, Noel	21h	17 mins
22.	Colsaet	21h	34 mins
23.	Filly	21h	35 mins
24.	Catteau	21h	35 mins
25.	Geay	21h	35 mins

55 Riders classified
Race distance - 467 kilometers (289.5 miles)
Winners average speed: 27.48 kph (16.9 mph)

---

1 "Pedards" means slow, amateur riders.

Chapter 4
Lyon, A Town Where They Talked About It

There was a rumor circulating on the finishing line that some riders had cheated. They turned towards Géo Lefèvre, he said that for the leaders it was impossible, because he had followed them. One man stood up to him and said the opposite. It was an occasion for an exchange of bitter words.

It was essential that the rumor be silenced. So Géo Lefèvre prepared a strong article for the newspaper.

"I can personally affirm that never has an event on the road been run more faithfully or more regularly than this one has been. On board Ouzou's Cotterreau motorcar, we really badgered the contestants. For example, Pothier, who had been dropped, was riding strongly and it seemed as if he was going to join the leading group. A kilometer in front of him was a motorcar. Another kilometer in front was a second motorcar. We reached these two speeding vehicles and we lay in ambush on a tight bend. If Pothier had cheated, he would have been caught, but Pothier did not cheat and it was all alone, with us behind him, that he was able to join his adversaries. As for Garin, from the time that he was alone in front with Pothier, we never left him, it was why we were able to put a troublemaker in his place. He was a firebrand who between Roanne and Lyon, was shouting at the top of his voice that he had seen Garin and Pothier cheating. It was his way of wantonly trying to harm the finest race that two men have ever ridden. How could the public do anything but shrug their shoulders at the protests of this troublemaker who was perturbed all the way to Lyon."

Henri Desgrange had decided to come to Lyon. It was his

responsibility to clear things up. To do this he had plenty of time as the race did not restart for a week. It was one of the peculiarities of this Tour de France. For the simple reason that they wanted spectators as much at Lyon as at Marseille, the riders were made to arrive on Sundays. This offered them plenty of rest. It also gave them ideas. It was necessary to remind them that they did not have the right to start any other race between two stages. This was no useless observation as several of them had already received offers from the Tete d'Or Velodrome at Lyon.

There were the complaints to be investigated. Being concerned to contain them, *L'Auto* pointed out that there were only two of them. The first was without any great foundation, but nevertheless they promised it would be investigated. As for the second, this was seen to be more serious as it consisted of written testimony. The riders concerned - so it was claimed - were going to be summoned to the branch office of *L'Auto* at Lyon. If there was any truth in the allegations, the said riders might just as well buy their train ticket to Paris without waiting!

In the meantime, it had been noted that Garin had improved on his previous year's time by thirty-eight minutes and Pothier by an astounding three hours.

Had "Father" Garin covered himself in more glory during the stage? Quite obviously, as for him, the route had been little more than a formality. In the eyes of the public, his image had certainly been embellished. And enriched with a new nickname. To the title of "The Little Chimney Sweep" and the more recent but little used "White Bulldog," had now been added "The Wild Boar." This name was due to Desgrange, who in the first half of the stage, had sensed that the ace had been attacked by a "veritable pack of hounds." This nickname gained widespread acceptance and temporarily gave birth to a zoological vision of the riders.

The day had scarcely arrived at the capital of the Gauls when the heroes were already on their feet. From 8 o'clock the three teammates of La Francaise, the Garin brothers and Pothier, were seen in the streets. Garin, easily recognized by the local people, wore a radiant expression on his face, but the contours of his moustache were a little droopy. To a resident who asked him if he was all right, he replied that he felt fresher than last year, in spite of the fact that it was a faster race and that they had been battling against a headwind.

But what were Géo Lefèvre and Georges Abran doing? Their time was taken up with meetings. Perhaps less for the journalist than for the delegate of *L'Auto* since he had to return to Paris. He had already arranged his timetable for the fast train which would steam its way back to the capital. He would only return on Saturday for the serious business of the race. In the meantime he would have seen Desgrange.

Abran stayed in Lyon with Miral who was charged with listening to the riders' gossip. Here Abran was virtually the embodiment of *L'Auto*. All organizational questions converged on him. As he had to establish a meeting place he had no hesitation in picking the terrace of the Cafe Riche. Just before midday, he was to be seen playing to perfection the role which had been delegated to him. He ordered a Pernod, sometimes two, while reminding the waiter that yellow was the color of the pages of *L'Auto*. It only remained for him to drink to the health of his newspaper.

Everyone had made plans for their week of rest. No one was a prisoner. On Tuesday, Garin used the day to go to Roanne. It was there that a fixed control had been set up during the first stage. The "Wild Boar" would thus have the chance to see it again but this time at his leisure. He was accompanied by his director, Delattre, who never missed a chance to show off his champion. However, Delattre was not very popular. Some spoke of him as being a crafty schemer. There was a rumor circulating to the effect that it was mainly he who was financing the Tour de France. Some insinuated that Desgrange would be far better off if he used only the means of his newspaper for the organization.

At Roanne, Garin spoke at length about the stage and it was noted that he perfectly remembered the details of the race and of the route. When he left his new-found friends, they knew the real reason for his journey; it was a fishing trip. For the ace of the road liked to use his rod and line.

Setting himself up on the river's bank was the best thing he could have done during the days when France was sweltering under a suffocating heat.

At Paris, the Faubourg Montmartre was melting and Desgrange was perspiring. Overheated by the worries *"a posteriori"* (at the end) of this first stage, he nevertheless had to smile at the dispatch which had come from Nemours concerning the policemen of the town. The incident which they had provoked was quite memorable. The police made it clear that they nursed not the slightest bad feeling towards the riders. According to them the affair was quite simple. Having not been officially warned that the race was passing through, they were surprised at the appearance of the cyclists. Their horses had taken fright and scattered across the road.

With this explanation, the constabulary saved its honor. The incident was closed.

Desgrange was still reveling in it when Géo Lefèvre arrived. The two men shut themselves in the office. No witnesses. No report.

Wednesday, Abran had hired six motorcars which he had loaded with riders. They were off to the park Tete d'Or for a photo call. The man with the big black cloth was Biot, working for *L'Auto*. He was taking pictures to his heart's content. Other regional colleagues were taking advantage of their good fortune and they too were using up their photographic plates. But the technique imposed constraints on the dailies who did not yet use the "similigravure" process and redrew the portraits.

Garin and his friends did not linger behind, they left for Saint-Etienne by road. Aucouturier was going to do the same, but not until the next day.

It was being acknowledged that *Le Velo*, although a fierce opponent of *L'Auto*, was beginning to take more and more notice of the Tour de France. So when Desgrange's paper came under attack from all sides for the irregularities of the event, this was their moment to strike! What do you expect when the complaints were being investigated and the critics rubbing their hands together? Among the opposition, of course, *Le Velo* would be able to unleash all of its venom.

Charles Ravaud, its cycling editor, although an old friend of Géo Lefèvre, had some good material to work with. He did not give full rein to his attacks, but adroitly used the accusations of others, namely readers who claimed to have been witnesses.

This article hit home. It took the form of a tale where the characters became incarnated in the bodies of animals. Inevitably we find a wild boar within the tale[1]:

'Once upon a time... there were some brave animals: a lion, a wild boar and a whole pack who decided to dispute a long, a very long and exacting race, divided into as many stages as would be necessary to get them lined up...

'A lame duck was charged with the regularity of the event that he wanted to be, so he said, sincere and loyal, and to this effect he caused one of his children to represent him. He had to follow all of the race in a beautiful motorcar in order to be sure that no fraud was committed.

'The unfortunate animals must receive no help from anybody.

'The day of the race arrived... Straight away the lion and the wild boar went to the front, but they raced so hard that they were hit by hunger, terrible hunger and they started to throw anguished looks at the motorcar.

'The duck's representative was so moved by this that he forgot his father's recommendations and did not draw back in the face of a crime. He cut into two a poor little chicken who had consented, with a number of others no doubt, to accompany him and threw the first half to the starving ones, who swallowed it instantly.

'These two became hungry again, and not being very grateful to their saviour, threatened to beat him up.

'Listening only to his courage, the duck's representative immediately braked and delegated a zebra, who was following the race as an amateur and on a motorcycle, to take the second half of the poor little chicken to the wild boar and the lion.

'The story does not tell us if he promised them any more.

'Well-filled, the two leaders regained their strength, and soon arrived at the finish, where the wild boar was able to precede his adversary, thanks to his habit of worming his way through the thickest undergrowth...'

So who were the real authors of this tale which was no doubt embellished even more by Ravaud? A group from Saint-Etienne, prosperous and highly respected people. They included a certain Grua, who was a merchant of silk; Gibert, a merchant of pianos and music; Clemengon, a cattle dealer; and Meunier, a manufacturer of wooden frames. As if by chance, there were four of them, just like the passengers in the car who shouted out to Garin and Pothier on the road to Lyon. But here, they were using more finesse to get their message across. You were left to wonder if Garin and the villagers by the side of the road had really heard the threats. Charles Ravaud revealed that this fable contained his part of the truth and that the authors, who lived in Saint-Etienne, were recognized by the organizers as troublemakers. Now going by the evidence on which he published the fable, he did not think badly of the quartet, even if the responsibility for what they said lay with them.

At the time when *Le Velo* appeared on the streets, Henri Desgrange was arriving in Lyon. He had travelled overnight. As he descended from the train he asked Abran, who had come to welcome him, to summon the riders who had been exposed to public condemnation.

"I want to see Chevalier. He was cheating, I'm sure of it! He'll pay for it. I'm also going to question Pothier, he deserves a reprimand."

Géo Lefèvre had most certainly delivered his report. The boss however had already "written his sermon," severity for Chevalier, indulgence for Pothier.

The dialogue with Chevalier was not very long. The man lacked any logical argument. His face was as impassive as it had been when he arrived at Lyon when he had not even smiled after receiving the bouquet for third place. He was unable to explain the reason why, after having been dropped so many times, he did not collapse but remained close to the leaders. He then admitted to having taken a series of lifts in a motorcar. When Desgrange told him that he was disqualified, he did not seem to understand. So Desgrange repeated: "Disqualified." Chevalier looked at him incredulously, got up, and left. The director of *L'Auto* had the impression that there was something not quite right with the man.

With Pothier, the discussion was more open. Desgrange knew him. He had come in second in the previous Tour.

"What happened, Lucien?"

The use of the Christian name already gave an indication of how favorably Desgrange regarded him. This made Pothier feel relaxed.

"You know my problems, M'sieur Desgrange?"

"Yes, the crash, the damaged bike, then the spare one you were given was not your size."

"It was a hard blow for me, as I was going so well."

"So was Aucouturier. He did not cheat. He remained at the back of the race."

"He was a long way back. I was able to rejoin and get back into the race."

"You rode behind a car?"

"Yes, Delattre's."

"Delattre, your team manager! But that's serious. You know the rules. I could put you out of the race for that!"

"Be lenient with me, M'sieur Desgrange."

"What a business!"

Desgrange did not hide his embarrassment. His gaze swept around the room several times. Then he said:

"I must be strict, Pothier. It's essential. I'll let you know my decision this evening."

The two men left each other without shaking hands. If Pothier was worried when he left, Desgrange had a choice to make - exclusion or fine? If it was a fine, it would have to be a very heavy one. Pothier had won 350F for his second place. Was it possible to go above that? He would have to see Delattre, his team manager.

The meeting took place in secret. As promised Pothier knew the verdict the same evening. 500F fine. He breathed again. He could continue the Tour de France. If everything went well, he could hope to finish second behind Garin and take home the 3,000F for the general classification.

It remained for the public to be informed. *L'Auto* on the tenth of July published a communique from Desgrange on the measures taken. As the case for the disqualified Chevalier was straightforward, so Pothier's case proved to be more involved.

"Chevalier was seen getting into a motorcar. At the time everybody was astonished to see him holding on to his third place, when it was believed he had retired. On learning the news I immediately disqualified him.

"I also imposed on Pothier a fine of 500F for having accepted, momentarily, pace from a motorcar in a way that brought dishonor and shame on him and those around him. If Chevalier's sin is impardonable, then that of Pothier can be excused. But what can be said about the conscience of those false sportsmen who have come in cold blood to help them cheat their comrades?

"And now, I am looking out for others on the second stage tonight."

He was not to be disappointed.

---

1 *Le Velo* July 9, 1904.

Chapter 5

The Dangers of "La Republique"

Lassagne, the man in charge of the control at the start, could not believe his eyes. This rider in his racing clothes, who was elbowing his way through the spectators, looked so much like Chevalier that he could have been his twin brother. The man approached. He reached for the pen.

"Your name?" Lassagne asked.

"Chevalier."

"I regret that you are not down on the list of starters."

The man went pale. "So, it's really true," he muttered.

Desgrange had said to him, he was disqualified. But he did not want to believe it.

He went away, without protesting, his bike in his hand, with a fixed look and his head lowered. A spectator insulted him. He did not reply. He disappeared around the corner. He would never be seen again.

It was close to 11 o'clock in the evening, on Sunday, the 10th of July, 1904. The Place de la Republique contained a huge crowd which buzzed with excitement. So, how many were packed in there? 10,000? 15,000? Some of them had not been able to get in the square and had to be content with just listening to the music from afar, in the Rue de la Republique. An instrumental music society, the "Standard of the Rhone," had already started on its repertoire two hours ago. With its brass and percussion it gave the evening a terrific atmosphere. The local population seemed to have an extraordinary need for distraction and a huge appetite for simple festivals.

The serious things were happening at the Cafe Riche. The

officials had been there since about four o'clock in the afternoon. The first task that had taken them there was to determine the starting time. Someone had put forward the idea that between Lyon and Marseille that it was right, when estimating the probable arrival time, to take the wind into account. The mistral (strong wind) in the Rhone valley, as was well known, could increase the speed of the riders considerably. So it was stipulated that, if there was a mistral, the start would be put back by two hours. So, everyone was waiting for the definitive dispatch. And finally it arrived -- no mistral.

What style and elegance it had, this 'Great Cafe Riche', bathed in the glow of its great gilded lights. Surrounded by two groups of flags, its terrace was ornamented by two huge banners borrowed from *L'Auto*. No one could be mistaken about the object of this concentration of people.

Desgrange was pacing up and down. He turned to Miral and said, "Go and hurry them up. We must start on time."

And the young journalist went to execute the order. The boss was never unpleasant with him, but all the same he had let him know that the copy which he had received in Paris was a little short. The lives of the riders during this week of rest at Lyon could have been developed and expanded upon. No, Miral had not shown himself to be "wordy" with his dispatch of only fifteen lines. Desgrange had not missed the opportunity to frown at his debut on the subject.

"What has happened to our 'Tour de France?' Where have they gone? To the devil, if I know anything about it, and for good reason. Lyon is no longer a town, it is a furnace! We are suffocating! So, our brave riders have been searching out the shade for some relief and, believe me, so have I, hiding like Tilyre behind the beneficial shade of my bedroom curtains."

For the moment, Miral was going to other bedrooms. He was looking for Garin and Aurcouturier at the Hotel of Russia where most of the riders were staying. All these gentlemen had expressed the greatest satisfaction with their stay. Some of them had even put on weight.

One by one our itinerant wayfarers arrived, impeccable in their laundered jackets and caps. But Aucouturier had not brought his striped jersey. The public applauded him but a more sustained ovation had already greeted the arrival of Garin.

Fifty-three competitors had just inscribed their signatures. It was 11:15 p.m., the register was closed. It remained for the riders to get to the start line at Jean-Jacques Rousseau Quay at Les Etroits. From here they left in one large group. They had been informed that they would be escorted by hundreds of cyclists. The junction took place. Nothing but bikes! And Venetian lanterns with their flickering orange glow. The harmony of the Standard of the Rhone was making itself heard in the distance. Its trumpets shone in the light of the flaming torches.

Georges Abran was already waiting for his flock. The last rider arrived. The roll-call could begin. One man did not reply immediately to his name, it was Antoine Faure. He was talking to his friends from Saint-Etienne.

"This time everything's fine, my eyes have not been burnt," he said. "In Paris a photographer did it intentionally, with his magnesium!"

"Don't worry, they can't keep trying to make you lose. You'll see, they're working for Garin. But we'll keep an eye out for trouble."

Abran had already raised his right arm, and solemnly asked, "Are you ready?"

The front rank nodded their agreement to their chief. A revolver shot rang out. The riders started. A cloud of dust enveloped them. Miral jumped in Ouzou's Cotterreau motorcar and Desgrange installed himself in a 24 horsepower De Dietrich driven by Dumont, another correspondent of *L'Auto*. Two other vehicles started their engines, a 40 horsepower Berliet and a 30 horsepower Chantiers de la Buire. It was almost a caravan!

It was noticed that Géo Lefèvre was not present. The boss had charged him with the coordination of dispatches. In Paris.

We are now en route for Rive-de-Gier and Saint-Etienne. In the middle of the night.

What had happened to Aucouturier, again? Here he was coming through Rive-de-Gier, after 35 kilometers, almost four minutes down. He was in a group of seven while Garin had passed through before with thirteen other companions.

Saint-Etienne. The town deserves more than a passing reference. For many years it had been a center for cycling. If Angers and Bordeaux, both well away from Paris, had taken turns to be manufacturing capitals of the bicycle and to put on races and demonstrate how well they could publicize the product; it was now Saint-Etienne that had taken the initiative. A very important firm was located there: "La Manufacture Francaise d'Armes et de Cycles" who was to make itself known to the public by adopting its telegragraphic address, "Manufrance." It produced a bicycle known everywhere in France, and throughout the world, "L'Hirondelle."Its catalogs were produced in several languages. But in cycling terms Saint-Etienne did not rely solely on L'Hirondelle, for a number of component manufacturers were based there as well.

At 5, rue de la Prefecture there was a small shop. It was run by Paul de Vivie, an innovator who made himself the apostle of "polymultiplication," which is to say, "gear changing." His own vocation was not racing but touring. He maintained to everyone, that if he was given a bike adapted to a particular road, flat or hilly, he would be able to cover long distances without being unduly tired. He claimed it and he proved it, regularly riding over very hilly roads, at more than fifty years of age, he regularly rode 240 kilometers in a day. His secret? The gear change. He possessed more than one of them, his shop had more than twenty types on display! Inexhaustable on the subject, he could offer, in this year of 1904, twelve monochain systems, eight systems with two chains, another with three chains and three devices which operated by the chain being moved. Moreover, as he was on good terms with the giant L'Hirondelle, and with its subsidiary, La Gauloise, he sold his monochain retro-direct system. This little world of "changing gears on the move" announced the beginnings of the clever derailleur, already implanted in some people's minds. This little world was in Saint-Etienne.

Paul de Vivie had other interests besides selling bikes. A lover of nature and of working up a good sweat, his main strength was above all his intellectual quality. From 1887, he founded his own review, *Le Cycliste Forezien*, shortly to become *Le Cycliste*. In his publication he tried to convince his readers of the futility of wearing themselves out with gears which were too large when you could climb hills with adequate gear ratios and then rediscover on the same bike gearing suitable for the flats. In his articles, which he signed "Velocio", he regularly proposed a confrontation between racing cyclists and cyclotourists over a mountainous route. In the accounts of his travels, he recounted with pleasure that when mixed groups of cyclists came together, it was always the cyclotourists who beat the racing cyclists over the top of the steeper climbs. Nothing could be more logical, the racers were penalized on the climbs by gears which were too large. But how could you convince the racing world? And especially the people from *L'Auto*?

He had not very far to come from his home, to see these paradoxical pedalers who, at the exit from the town, were going to confront the Col du Grand Bois with gears more suited to flat roads.

There was a lot of light at the Grand Cafe Moderne at 6 Rue du Montat. And a lot of people. The correspondent of *L'Auto* had prepared things very well with the help of three racing clubs from the town. And he had taken on a third society dedicated to touring, the "Club Cycliste Excursioniste," to help mark the route. They were situated 200 meters from there, equipped with Bengal lanterns.

"Attention!" A warning bell rang out at the same time as glow from the pink and green lanterns lit the night. Everyone rushed to the front of the cafe. A rider came through. Alone. It was not Garin. It was Faure, the local man. The crowd quivered with excitement and some of them almost cried with joy. The brave little man! He signed the register and began again almost immediately. He had a sealed bike, so he had to keep the same gear. "Velocio" smiled. With irony, no doubt.

More than a minute later, Garin arrived; he had let the man go just before the town. Perhaps he had given his permission to Faure so that he could go through first. The welcome was somewhat cold. He was whistled at and even received a few insults. No question of Garin hanging around. Two more minutes passed before a group of another 20 riders appeared; Pothier, Cèsar Garin and others. Aucouturier was with them. Each one of them kept the same bike with the gear for the flat roads. Here, the spectators were impressed. They knew that higher up on the Cote de Planfoy, the gradient was steep. Some bikes were equipped with gears of more than six meters! "Velocio" stayed quiet, he was not part of this little world. In a future article he took the opportunity to compare this situation with that of one of his friends who he had led up a mountain and who had a gear of 6.30 meters and who of course came to a stop.

"He has since become one of the most convinced partisans of

multiple-geared machines, reducing year by year his smallest gear of 3.65 meters to 3.25 meters and finally to 2.70 meters, although his muscles still permitted him, when he pleased, to climb up the ten kilometer ascension of the Col du Grand Bois with its average gradient of over six percent, with a gear of 6.60 meters, after the fashion of the riders of the Tour de France, keyed up with excitement by *L'Auto* which was wary of sending them to the climbs of the Echarasson, to the Galibier and to the Ventoux, where perhaps they too would find their road to Hell."

Garin and Aucouturier would probably have to be content with 5.85 meters. But you never know, perhaps they were even crazier than they seemed.

For the moment a regrouping took place on the climb. Some of the lesser-known riders put their feet to the ground. But the Garins, the Faures, the Pothiers, the Aucouturiers, and the Gerbis were climbing strongly. Fortunately, some respite was to be offered further up, on the plateau of La Republique. So Garin was looking towards the summit. The day was breaking slowly, but the night was no longer so dense. Pothier was climbing easily alongside his leader.

Suddenly Faure attacked.

"Let him go, his fans must be at the top," Garin thought. "Look, Gerbi wants to go as well, he's trying to catch the man from Saint-Etienne. For me everything's all right, one last climb and there's the summit."

But who were all these people blocking the road? Faure threaded his way through them. He was recognized and applauded. Then arms were raised. With clubs. Pothier avoided the blows and went through on Faure's wheel. Gerbi was thrown to the ground. He had taken a blow on the back of his neck. He had been struck on his fingers. He screamed with pain.

Maurice Garin fell as well, an enormous stick hit him on his right arm. Cèsar Garin was not spared either. A chorus of yells and cries of rage was heard. And the motorcars, were they going to come and put a stop to this carnage? Pistol shots rang out! They came from Desgrange's vehicle. The hooligans ran away. They were pursued to the edge of the woods. The gunfire increased.

Gerbi and Garin were still on the ground when Desgrange came up to them, his revolver still smoking.

"Nothing too serious?" he shouted.

His remarks were addressed to both men, but above all to his leader, Garin.

"If my arm's not broken, I'll be able to get going again. But I don't know how well I'll do. See what they did to Gerbi."

The unfortunate Gerbi was unable to get up. He was really hurt. He would have to be helped to restart.

"What a bunch of savages!" said Desgrange to his driver. "Just to think that we did not have to come through Saint-Etienne and that it was to please them that we did so. We will never come back here again. In any case I'm going to put in a complaint, for if we let them get away with it, people like that are going to kill cycle sport."

Maurice Garin was already back on his bicycle. Cèsar was with him. In the first bends of the descent his usual assurance was lacking. His arm was hurting him a lot... No matter, risks had to be taken! The two men caught Josselin first. Then Lombard. Then Cornet. And this group could see a cloud of dust in the distance. It then engulfed Aucouturier and the others.

At Annonay, an official check-point had been established. A dozen riders were seen to be together. Garin was one of them on the list. Was the incident on the Col du Grand Bois going to have any consequences?

Gerbi was suffering too much! His finger had been broken. He could not hold his handlebars properly. He was scarcely able to avoid the holes in the road. And the roads around here were not of good quality. Garin turned around for a moment, Gerbi had disappeared. At Tournon, he learned that the Italian had retired. It could easily have happened to him, Maurice Garin, last year's winner of the Tour de France.

He asked Faure about his aggressors: "Did you know any of them back there?"

"No," he replied, "but I think they may have been miners, or people who lead a hard life. They wanted to let off steam. The local papers have been saying that the winner had been chosen before the start. And that he was called Garin. There are fans who think a lot of me."

"But that's all crazy. On an event as long as this it's impossible to designate a winner in advance. All sorts of things could happen to me just as they have to Aucouturier. Many others could prove to be much stronger than I am. I have got to go and win my victory."

The elder Garin was visibly outraged. But he did not hold this incident against Faure who was probably not directly involved, even if he knew that he had 'warmed up' his supporters during the week of rest which he had spent at Saint-Etienne.

The riders had eased up, which explained their chatter. They conversed quietly. The route traversed the Ardeche bank of the river Rhone. Dortignacq and Catteau even stopped to pilfer some fruit. There was no shortage of peaches.

Tournon, the one hundred and twenty-sixth kilometer. Eleven riders arrived in the leading group and passed through the flying control: Maurice and Cèsar Garin, Pothier, Aucouturier, Catteau, Lombard, Frederick, Dortignacq, Faure, Chaput and Cornet. Three more arrived fifteen minutes later. The spectators had the general impression that all of the men were not riding too hard. They were quickly recovering from their climb up the Col du Grand Bois but above all they were saving their strength, for it was going to be hot, and there were no signs of clouds in the sky.

At Valence, they were required to sign in. In such a short distance there was no change among the race leaders. Garin took his time. He passed a sponge over his face and greedily swallowed his soup. He had difficulty in lifting his elbow. His arm was painful. He carried traces of bruises and swelling. Delattre, his team manager, was worried about him. While the others were busy he took him to one side to question Garin. "Do you think you can hold on?"

"Yes, if the speed is not too high."

"Get Pothier and Cèsar to slow the pace a bit."

"We'll see what we can do."

He could not say anymore. Aucouturier had just restarted, all the other riders were back on the road, except Catteau, who hung back. He was tired and could only just hang on to the wheel in front.

The festival of dust restarted. In the direction of Montelimar.

"It's not going to be a piece of nougat with the heat we are expecting," said Lombard, the man from Liege. He was joking in order to reassure himself, surprised to still be with the best at this point in the race. The man was holding the position of leader of the riders with the sealed machines. He was in front of Faure and Cornet. For him it was a new and delightful adventure.

In the city of sweetmeats, there were ten men in the leading group. All of the favorites were among them. Someone disclosed that there were still close to 200 kilometers to cover. The heat had not yet reached its full intensity, the clocks showed that it was just after 8 o'clock in the morning. No rider seemed to have suffered from lack of sleep during the night. Most of them had managed a siesta before the start and had drank a lot of coffee during the night. Some of them had taken caffeine tablets and at one time or another had consumed glassfuls of cola. Frederick made no attempt to hide it. The powers of cola were spoken highly of in the journals, it was sold in the form of powder or pastilles. The Hirondelle catalog offered it amid the pages of caps, pumps, oil cans and shoes. These pastilles, the manufacturers claimed, "gave resistance to fatigue, alleviated shortness of breath and gave an agreeable freshness to the mouth." As for the powder, "a complete and pure extract from the cola nut, it has over chocolate and cocoa, the advantage of being more nourishing while at the same time being easier to digest. It is the most perfect antidote to exhaustion and the most economic one." Like that which was prepared in milk, and given to children. Aucouturier himself, preferred it in wine. As for Garin, no one knew. Did he put it in his soup?

Assuredly it was Frederick who proved to be the greatest consumer of these "antidotes to exhaustion."

For the moment it was this same Frederick who was at the front of the group for most of the time, with Aucouturier and Maurice Garin. The "Little Chimney Sweep" had this to say, "Careful, it's going to be very hot. We must be careful. Don't go too hard in the hills. If everyone does his bit, we'll all be together at Marseilles, and that will benefit all of us."

The minor riders, Cornet, Lombard, Chaput and Dortignacq had immediately agreed with "father" Maurice. For them it meant they had the opportunity for him to take them with him to the finish. They would do their work and the strength of the group would do the rest. A regular pace but sufficiently rapid to put them out of reach of the others. Aucouturier was in agreement. He was benefitting from a well structured group and had been spared the incidents which had handicapped him between Paris and Lyon. He was faster than any of them and knew how to get past them in the final straight. When you are the best of the bunch, you must know how to bide your time. One single man was keeping to himself, but holding his line very carefully, Faure. He never went to the front.

Withdrawn into himself, he was keeping totally silent and visibly upset. That affair in the Col du Grand Bois was a bad one!

And behind? It was not yet the complete disorder which we had seen on the first day. At Montelimar, a group of about twenty came through followed by another two or three. They were half an hour and one hour down.

Jean Miral, driving in the Cotterreau motorcar, had just observed Payan, a rider from Ales. He had been obstinately sitting on the wheel of an unknown cyclist. He was reminded that pacers were not allowed. So the stranger was sent on his way.

The heat by now was becoming exhausting. You could even say that the wind, which was coming from the South was making it worse, as if the heat from the Sahara had not been dissipated at all when crossing the Mediterranean.

"It's the hot wind from hell!" said Pothier.

The "Butcher of Sens" was now doing most of the work. The Swiss Frederick was showing signs of weakness. Sometimes he was even seen behind Faure. On the climbs, he often lost contact but rejoined on the flat roads, using all his strength.

At the Avignon control, at ll:20 a.m., he was still with the group. While Garin was swigging down his soup and Pothier was biting into a cutlet, he paid a visit to the toilets. An emergency? The others did not stay here for so long. In three minutes everything was settled. Most of the "non-sealed" riders had even changed their bikes. Some of them to take advantage of better tires, others for bigger gears. Was this the area where Lombard made his mistake? Riding on a sealed machine, he had no right to ride any other bike and could not even change a wheel. It was written into the rules. So it was inevitable that at the finish, the rider from Liege would be struck off the list of "Poinconnes."

Things were going badly for Frederick. On the road to Lambesc, where a flying control had been established, he was vomiting.

"I must have a touch of sunstroke," he declared.

The bunch saw him stop at a fountain and stick his head in the water. The pedalers had already disappeared when he stretched out in the shade. Was he going to retire? The idea had occurred to him as his strength had left him and his heart was racing.

In front, no one thought about feeling sorry for him. He was a good comrade and an experienced rider, but he had the reputation of overdoing the "stimulants." The young Cornet, thinking about the cause of the incident, realized that the time had come to place a white handkerchief over the back of his neck. However, none of the riders had yet taken their tights off. Cèsar Garin would like to have done so but his elder brother dissuaded him from doing so.

"Don't do that! You remember my Paris-Brest-Paris? I won because I kept them on and Lesna lost because he took them off. The sun will wreak havoc on your legs."

The incident had taken place three years previously, but Maurice Garin never tired of reminding his younger brother of it.

In the Cotterreau, Miral was having strong words with Payan, who was tired and refused to leave the slipstream of his pacer.

"Payan, I'm warning you one last time, if you don't respect the rules, you'll be disqualified!"

The man from Ales raised his right arm and pulled it back to his shoulders. As the gesture was not accompanied with any comment, it could be equally interpreted in a violent or a moderate manner. From "We'll see!" to "Just try it!" by way of "I don't give a damn about your silly rules."

An exasperated Miral stopped the motorcar. Desgrange, who was behind at the time, was warned when he came through. He drew level with Payan, noted that he was still sheltered and called out to him, "Payan! You've already been warned four times. Now I'm telling you officially: you will not be classified at the finish!"

Then he accelerated away to the front of the race.

The flying control at Lambesc was installed in the Cafe de l'Union, on the route national in the shade of the plane trees. The riders did not have to stop. But it was so hot! They all rushed to the fountain to cool themselves off.

At Aix-en-Provence, 20 kilometers further on, with their hollow faces made red by the sun, the crowd was considerable. The women were using their parasols. The control was completed at the Velodrome de Provence, where a fine reunion had been organized. Nine riders signed in as one man at this 343rd kilometer point. The gaps did not seem to be enormous. One man was holding on behind the leaders, Catteau. He came through less than half an hour down, which seemed to indicate that the top men were not setting a furious pace. An hour behind Garin and associates, were to be found Beaugendre, Gabory and... Payan. The rider was counting on reaching Marseille. The unfortunate Frederick, who had a good record in cycle racing, was clocked in two and a half hours after the leaders. Many thought that he had retired. No, he had recuperated a bit in the shade, taken a little food, and then rode slowly along the road. And now, at Aix, he stopped for more rest.

The exact location of the finish of the stage was not entirely clear. The preliminary communique of *L'Auto* was categoric. "The finish at Marseille will be at the Larcheveque Velodrome.

"It is at this same velodrome that the time counting towards the general classifications of the Tour de France will be taken.

"Nevertheless, an inspector will be established like last year at Saint-Antoine, at the Cafe du Murier, the route between Saint-Antoine and the velodrome being neutralized."

"At Saint Antoine, each rider will receive a card bearing his exact time of arrival, he will have to present the card on arrival at the velodrome and will only be allowed to enter the track exactly 60 minutes after his arrival at Saint-Antoine. The neutralization, previously set at 30 minutes, has been increased to 60 minutes.

"All the riders arriving after 7:30 p.m. at Saint-Antoine will be exempted from going to the velodrome. Sixty minutes will simply be added to their time, then two minutes for the final kilometer from which they will have been exempted."

The Larcheveque Velodrome was filled with a jubilant crowd. A superb supporting program with half a dozen different races had been organized. The prestigious sprinter Jacquelin was top of the bill. Regarding our "Tourers de France," they were invited to complete their final kilometer on the track and the best of them would receive 100F and 50F respectively.

Before then, they had to arrive at Saint-Antoine. But it was here that things started to go wrong. The people charged with the maintenance of order recommended that the finish should be judged at Saint-Antoine and no longer at the Larchevque Velodrome, ten kilometers away and in the center of town. It was believed that the managers of the velodrome had made no arrangements to judge the finish on their track. Quite obviously, everyone was tired, the organizers as much as the riders. Last year the finish had taken place here, at Saint-Antoine. But were they forgetting that this year, nine riders were in contention for the stage prize and you needed the best of conditions for the sprint? At the very least it was necessary to make these changes known.

It was Desgrange himself who took care of it. Having arrived at Saint-Antoine in the De Dietrich motorcar driven by Dumont, while the riders were not far behind, he set out again. One kilometer from there, he took up a prominent position and, with the help of a megaphone, made his announcement:

"Attention! Attention! There is a major change. The official classification will be at Saint-Antoine and not at the velodrome!"

Then doubting that it had sunk in and seeing the surprised look of incomprehension on the faces of the riders, he repeated the same phrase. It did not stop Dortignacq from asking Pothier the question, "What did he say?"

And the other replied between his teeth, as he forced his way onto Aucouturier's wheel, who he wanted to watch. "Finish at Saint-Antoine."

And Dortignacq started to tear along. Here he was at the front, preceding Chaput, Pothier, and Aucouturier. Was this the finishing line already? A banner was stretched across the road lined with spectators. That's it! That's the line. What happiness! Dortignac has won. He sits up. Chaput too. Pothier, Aucouturier and a few others do not slow down.

Three men are now at the front: Aucouturier, Cèsar Garin and Pothier. Suddenly there was a bend close to the finish. The riders get "mixed up." It looks like they are going to fall. Fortunately the crash is avoided. The finishing order remains the same, Aucouturier is declared the winner.

Dortignacq is dismayed. He protests. Nobody wants to listen to him. It was Aucouturier who was first across the line, they tell him.

"But what line?" he asks.

By way of reply, he was told that they had now to go to the velodrome, situated on the Avenue du Prado.

The riders did not have a lot of time at their disposal before their next performance at the Larcheveque Velodrome. They had a quick wash without as much as changing their clothing. Some of them were hungry and thirsty. Milk was drunk and fruit was eaten. One rider was biting into some hard-boiled eggs when Abran came to announce, "Gentlemen, we must go. The cars are ready."

Pothier took the helmet that was offered him. It was designed for a automobile racers and had earpieces. Was he totally insensitive to the heat which was almost tropical on this afternoon? Like his eight comrades he climbed into one of the motorcars.

A timetable had been arranged. The riders could not enter the velodrome until one hour had elapsed after their arrival at Saint-Antoine.

Abran and the timekeepers at the track were being vigilant. They kept looking at their watches. It was time. They liberated the nine men. Straight away, Aucouturier went flat out. It's not possible! This man has not just ridden 370 kilometers, the public thought. Dortignacq held on to his wheel. This man was good! But, in the last 100 meters, "The Terrible" gained several lengths on him. Times for the first two: 1 minute 16 seconds and 1 minute, 17 seconds for one kilometer.

This second place on the track did not satisfy Dortignacq, it only brought him 50F while the stage itself would have enlarged his wallet by 500F. Right up until Paris he was to contest the stage result.

Undoubtedly, improvisation was the mark of this Tour de France. If *L'Auto* made no mention of it, the provincial press and Le Velo showed themselves to be in a more critical state of mind.

It was true that *Le Velo* was not in the business of bestowing presents on its rival. This is the way it analyzed the finish at Saint-Antoine:

"A number of protests have arisen, following the classification of the second stage of the Tour de France at Marseille.

"Our corespondent wrote to us on the subject:

"The organization here was absolutely pitiful. All week it had been agreed that the finish would be judged at the Larcheveque Velodrome and on Sunday, without anybody being warned, it was decided that it would take place at Saint Antoine.

"The order of finishing was taken haphazardly. Aucouturier was classified first in spite of the indignant protests of the spectators, who had all seen Dortignacq precede him by two lengths.

"Dortignacq addressed to all the newspapers of Marseille a letter of complaint protesting about the unjust measure taken against him."

Another daily, *Le Petit Provencal*, joined him in his remarks. "The finish at Marseille had been fixed at Saint-Antoine. But as a consequence of the crowds of inquisitive onlookers, and it must be said also by fault of a defective organization, they were obliged to move the control forward along the road about 200 meters from

Saint-Antoine, by the canal.

"The arrival of the leading group, at 3:39 p.m., was followed by regretable incidents which justly aroused public protest. It was a modest and little-known rider - but for all that no less courageous, in fact quite the contrary - who finished first at the control, Dortignacq. In spite of everything, the commissioners and the organizers of the previous race, believed they had the right not to award him the first place, and it was Aucouturier who was declared winner in his place, although he had certainly been fourth between Chaput and Pothier."

This same newspaper also revealed the anomaly of the official timekeeping of the finish, announced at the velodrome and finally held at Saint-Antoine.

While we are consulting the press, it must be said that none of them took Garin's injury into account. No mention at all was made of the importance of his handicap. After the Col du Grand Bois, he was never able to pull on the handlebars in the way that he would have wished. Instead of aggression, he was obliged to remain on the defensive. Fortunately, none of his adversaries dropped him. Which is to say that he limited the damage superbly. It was a mark of his professionalism. Pothier was a hostage to the situation, in as much as, being a teammate he could not attack Maurice. In the face of the evidence, the first place should have passed on to him. But Delattre, the team manager of La Francaise, had urged him to do nothing. Advertising based on a cheat who had become leader, would not have been in the best interests of the company.

Without this injury, "The Little Chimney Sweep" would no doubt have demonstrated his usual brilliance and the fight would have been ferocious between him and "The Terrible." Who would have been able to hang on to them? Pothier at most. It was very important for *L'Auto* to give news of Garin and to reassure public opinion. The health of this Tour de France depended on Garin. Desgrange pointed out that the "ace" had had his injury examined and that, although his arm was inflamed, he should be able to restart. For readers of *L'Auto*, the Tour de France will continue to be of interest, Garin will still be there, determined to demonstrate his bravery and to impose his class as a great roadman on the others!

Here are the results of Stage 2 - Lyon - Marseille:

1. Aucouturier   Bicycle: Peugeot
                 Tires: Michelin
      Average speed: 25.148 kph...... 15h 09 min

  2. Garin, Cèsar .... 15h 09 min
  3. Pothier .... 15h 09 min
  4. Garin, Maurice .... 15h 09 min
  5. Faure .... 15h 09 min
  6. Lombard .... 15h 09 min
  7. Cornet .... 15h 09 min
  8. Dortignacq .... 15h 09 min
  9. Chaput .... 15h 09 min
10. Catteau .... 15h 49 min
11. Beaugendre .... 16h 31 min
12. Gabory .... 16h 31 min
13. Samson .... 16h 33 min
14. Ventresque 17h
15. Dargassies .... 17h 21 min
16. Geay .... 17h 38 min
17. Prèvost, Charles .... 17h 41 min
18. Saget .... 18h 02 min
19. Paret .... 18h 03 min
20. Colas .... 18h 03 min
21. Frederick .... 18h 11 min

Race distance: 381 K (236.2 miles)
Winner's average speed = 25.148 kph (15.59 mph)

Payan, although he arrived at the same time as Beaugendre and Gabory, was not classified. Desgrange did not go back on his decision.

The general classification comprised no more than forty-one riders. The first ten were:

  1. Garin, Maurice .... 32h 16 min 07s
  2. Pothier .... 32h 16 min 31s
  3. Garin, Cèsar .... 32h 21 min

4.	Lombard	32h 21 min
5.	Faure	34h 19 min
6.	Beaugendre	34h 43 min
7.	Aucouturier	34h 46 min
8.	Cornet	34h 46 min
9.	Dortignacq	35h 38 min
10.	Frederick	35h 58 min

Would the third stage, the exhausting Marseille-Toulouse, 424 kilometers, be less eventful than the second? The supporters of Payan at Ales were outraged by the disqualification which had struck their fellow citizen, while Pother had been given a mere fine for the same offense. They threatened to disrupt the control at Nimes. Would they carry out their threat? Some of the top riders started to contemplate whether or not they should start with revolvers.

Chapter 6
Marseille - Toulouse

There had been an essential change for this third stage in the length of time allowed for rest and recovery before the race resumed. If the first and second acts had been separated by a week, now only three days had been granted to the riders to dress their wounds and recover their strength. The two locations used for the finish of the last stage, the Larcheveque Velodrome and the village of Saint-Antoine, were used again for the start. Spectators were waiting for the riders at the velodrome for the signing-in ceremony and then at Saint-Antoine for the official send off.

On Wednesday from 6:00 p.m., while the first contestants came to pick up their armbands, an enormous crowd was pressing around the edge of the track. The riders from the north paid no more attention to the singing accents of these gawking onlookers who were calling out to them. For three days they had been in the heart of the metropolis, soaking up the excitement of the hustle and bustle. Some of them had taken advantage of the boat excursions. The least daring only went as far as the Chateau d'If, while others went all the way to the rocky inlet of Cassis. A believer went to burn a candle at the cathedral of Notre-Dame-de-la-Garde. "On the road, you need to be protected," he said to those astonished by his devotion. For the riders, these three days were consecrated to rest and avoiding the heat which was strangling the city.

It was already known that Frederick had not recovered. People had been astonished by his absence from the velodrome. The modest rider, Alibert Leroy, also helped to swell the ranks of the defectors. He paid his tribute to the road in another way. While he was "slogging away" near Aix, in the hope of arriving at Marseille, a vehicle devoid of any sort of light hit him and threw him to the ground. He was driven to the hospital where he still remained. Three other riders had also given up, Romaine Lardillier, Deflotiere and Debalade. Payan, the eliminated, could no longer represent Gard, the county of his birth. Strong rumors were circulating that due to his exclusion, things were going to be very hot when the race reached Nimes.

In the morning, *L'Auto* had published a letter signed by the Garin brothers, Pothier, Daumain, Catteau and Jousselin, about the events on the Col du Grand Bois and the threats uttered from the motorcar which had cut across them before Lyon.

Quite obviously this Tour de France was raising high passion.

Few riders used their bikes to get to Saint-Antoine where the sealed machines were checked for a second time. Abran was already waiting, ready to give the starting signal. He too had spent three good days. He was as elegant as ever. While his large hat had proved its value, protecting him from the sun, he had never considered giving up his big bow tie. As for his liking for strong drink, his friends had noticed on several occasions that he had pronounced an energetic "no" followed by a friendly "thank you." Just imagine the number of offers he would have received in this "Pernod capitol"!

As straight as a flagstaff and sweating like a horse in his three piece suit, Abran, with his stentorian voice, had given his last orders. And the convoy pulled away, as always in a cloud of dust.

Henri Desgrange was not among them. He had gone back to Paris, taking advantage of the express train laid on for the Bay of Tunis. For several days he had been very moody. He found himself torn between an obligation to clamp down on those who were cheating and the worry of offending a part of the public who were demanding sanctions against those guilty of mere trifles. "Some local cyclists, for the vain glory of having ridden 200 meters with the leading group, place themselves at the front, in spite of the protests of the riders themselves, the crowd sees them as the forbidden followers and claim that fraud is being committed.

"Consequently, the crowd, which on the one hand exaggerates the strictness of our rules, on the other hand also exaggerates the tolerance with which the rules must be administered in a race run on the road, which belongs to everyone."

Géo Lefèvre, in person, was back on the race, helped by Jean Miral. He alerted the town of Nimes so that the services of law and order could be reinforced.

It was still daylight on this Wednesday evening at 9 o'clock. The riders would just have time to get used to the roads before plunging into the tunnel of the night. Some delighted in playing the role of night hawks. No, it was not that they were insomniacs, but they knew that the Mediterranean sun would not be beating down on them when it was the moon that occupied the sky.

This evening was no ordinary one. It preceded the national holiday of the 14th of July, one of the rare occasions when the workers laid down their tools. As the riders passed from village to village they saw a series of lively activities. With the night, which had finally arrived as the race went through Vitrolles, the celebrations had taken on a new scale. The light, normally to be seen in only miserly amounts, shone forth everywhere. The "fairy" of electricity was in competition with the gas lamps.

At Salon-de-Provence, everyone was waiting for the riders at the first fixed control. Anxiety was growing. There had not been any news of the leading group. They must be quite close by now. The news finally came. The start had been put back by half an hour. However, the information did not have the effect of totally removing the worries for the directors of the Salon Velo, in charge of the control point. The festivities taking place in town did not always lead only to good fortune and happiness. The jubilation aroused by the torchlight procession was causing problems. The enthusiastic crowd spilled off into most of the town and onto the route of the race. What a crush! Even the mossy fountain disappeared from view under the weight of the revelers. How would the riders get through? Fortunately, the late start meant that there was time to restore order. The procession of revelers went on its way and the riders would be able to arrive in relative calm.

At 10:40 p.m., here they were. Frenzied and fanatical! They all wanted to sign in at the same time. Pothier managed to seize the pen first. Then it was the turn of Garin and the others. A quick count revealed that there were 20 of them.

Already they were back on the road, in the Mediterranean silence. The night was balmy. The Provence sky revealed myriads of stars. It was always the top men who were leading this front group. The lesser-known riders were quite satisfied to just stay on their wheels. The speed was a steady 30 kph. The road was completely flat and somewhat stoney, so it offered little relief. The riders were happy that the road had few ruts and that the farm carts had not worn too many deep grooves in the surface. The best precaution was to fit their bicycles with wide tires. But the pace suffered because of it.

The race reached Ales. Eighty-eight kilometers had been covered in a little more than three hours. Garin and his rivals received loud cheers, but they had no wish to slow down. Firstly. because it was a race that they were riding, but also because some children were throwing firecrackers at them. It was the 14th of July, Bastille Day, and they were determined to have some fun.

The Cotterreau motorcar preceded this little pedaling world, with Lefèvre and Miral on board, while Rivierre closed the ranks on his motorbike. He made a fuss, this "Father Rivierre", with his "Special Motorcycle." Designed as a delivery tricycle, it contained a series of original features. The public recognized him as the triple winner of the Bordeaux-Paris and he remained close to their hearts. This made him particularly happy and he lost no opportunity to promote himself, already thinking of the Motor Show where he was to have his own stand. There he would be able to show his new hub, "the only one which would allow you to start on a hill without pedaling, the only one which would allow a motor-tricycle to be used in congested areas and the only one with two gears and a progressive clutch." Already, with his associates, he had sketched out the advertisements which he would be placing in *L'Auto* and *Le Velo,* for as long as the latter title continued to appear. For all was not well at the newspaper's headquarters at 2 Rue Meyerbeer. The circulation was in a free fall. They were forced to make drastic cutbacks. It was for this reason that their special envoy on the Tour de France went no further than Villeneuve-Saint-Georges. They had to be content with managing the dispatches and drawing on information in the regional press. Fortunately, a critical look uncovered things here and there while *L'Auto* could not escape from its subjectivity as the organizer.

For the moment, in the middle of the night, the men were pedaling in the direction of Nimes. One of them put his hand in the bag on his handlebars: his revolver was still there. It meant extra weight to carry, but with this firearm, he felt much safer. He often took it when he went training alone in the provinces. The roads were not safe. Once, the local people wanted to cause trouble, for a chicken that he had run over. Another time, he had to shoot a dog who had bitten him and continued to attack him. How many generations of dogs would it take before they understood what a cyclist was?

Though there were a large number of policemen in Nimes, all keeping a high profile, everything seemed to be fine in the town, in spite of the rumors which made everyone fear the worst. An attack was expected at the entry to or the exit from town, or perhaps on a sharp bend or a hill. It was in such a situation that a revolver would become useful. To the riders these threats appeared to be totally unjust, they personally had nothing to do with the decisions and sanctions of the organizers. It was not they who had disqualified Payan.

They were turning these questions over in their mind, some 20 kilometers from the county town of the Gard, when one of them shouted out, "Puncture!"

It was Chaput, the man from Lyon. What rotten luck, a nail. Another rider stopped alongside him. The other rider was going to help him. No, he had punctured as well. It was Dortignacq. The road was covered in nails. New ones whose points shone in the light of the moon. Two other riders fell victim to the same sabotage.

By good fortune, Garin and the others at the head of the general classification were able to avoid this malevolence. As they rode along they congratulated themselves that they had avoided the problems. As the first glow of the lights of Nimes appeared in the distance, Aucouturier said, "It's O.K. men, they wouldn't dare attack us in the town. But we'll have to be on our guard as we leave it."

But like all his companions, he had not taken into account a certain welcoming committee. He did not know that Payan was at the control with a large number of people, his friends from the Moto Velo Club of Alais and a number of his fellow citizens. The people certainly did not look like peaceful spectators. Clearly they were all very angry.

"You have no right," Payan shouted at those from *L'Auto*, Lefèvre, Miral and the driver. "I was not cheating! My name is not Pothier or Aucouturier, I didn't ride behind a car!"

It was the time and place to keep quiet, but Miral shouted back, "You were warned. You cannot take any shelter behind cyclists!"

Straight away, the barriers were toppled over and the crowd surged over them. The handful of policemen could do nothing. Dozens of excited citizens rushed toward the control tables.

A man next to Payan, with his cap on the side of his head, screamed,
"We're going to stop the race and you're going to have a really rough time!"

The impact was immediate and one of the controllers closed his register and took refuge in the cafe. Two or three thousand indignant people surrounded the block. The atmosphere became even more heated. Quite obviously the people from Nimes were not all in agreement with those from Ales.

"Be reasonable, you can't stop a race like the Tour de France in order to defend a rider who has not respected the rules. Don't act like a bunch of thugs," said someone who could only have come from the town.

"Thugs?" You could not say that here. A big strapping man hit him with a huge punch and the recipient collapsed onto one of the fallen barriers. Stones were thrown and one of them hit the controller. The police constables proved unable to control the situation.

From the back of the crowd there came a rumor that the road was barred at the exit to the town. People looked at each other incredulously. Was this to become a complete riot? Was it true that someone pointed to Lefèvre and his associates and cried out: "Kill them!" Some believed that they had heard it. It was at this precise moment that the trumpet rang out. This trident call, used to announce the arrival of the riders, continued its prearranged ritual and was in total contrast to the agitation at the checkpoint. It had the effect of calming things down, just giving the riders the time to get to the check-in tables, then the fury restarted. Dozens of madmen, waving their fists, threw themselves at the cyclists. Garin succeeded in getting away, but not without first receiving a fist in his face and taking a blow on his right leg. For Pothier, it was his left arm that caught it. He screamed in pain.

Aucouturier was struggling in the middle of the tumult. "Let me through!" he insisted.

It was then that he received a blow on the shoulder. His moustache quivered. He turned around, his face red with anger. In a flash, he was transformed into a boxer. He threw an uppercut. But other hooligans were approaching.

"Let me pass, for God's sake!"

They saw him grab his bike and twirl it around his head. That got him free. Jousselin, a quiet and gentle rider, found himself caught between two louts. Surprisingly, these two suddenly drew back. They had just heard the explosion of a firearm. This detonation came from the motorcar belonging to *L'Auto*. It was stopped 50 meters from the control for the simple reason that one of its tires had been pierced by a knife and it had settled onto its rim. So as to free his little team, it was Miral who had fired into the air.

The frenzied crowd finally drew aside. Payan approached the motorcar. With a strained face, he directed a worried look at Géo Lefèvre. His head moved twice, then he said, "I didn't want this. My friends have gone too far. I am sorry."

"It's all right, let us leave," replied Lefèvre, who could see no point in punishing him while at the same time realizing that his passage was now free.

Miral fired some more shots into the air. Ouzou let the clutch in very gently, he did not want to damage his punctured tires. At the first crossroads, he decided to take a different road to avoid the louts at the exit from the town. Fortunately, this chauffeur, who, in Paris, as we know, ran a garage, had brought one of his apprentices with him. With Miral, it took three pairs of hands to repair the car. During this time, Lefèvre was attempting to write the dispatch that he was going to telegraph from Montpellier. Imagine what Desgrange would be like when he received it at the Faubourg Montmartre! His Tour de France was turning into a disaster!

Riders and officials succeeded in avoiding the traps which had been prepared for them as they left Nimes. In the countryside, silent and dark, everyone tried to calm down. For the riders, the memory of the aggression was dissipated by the act of pedaling. Paradoxically, the first to arrive, although they had received some blows, had suffered less from the disorganization of the control than the ones who followed them. These men presented themselves at the heart of an incredible turmoil and indescribable congestion.

Cèsar Garin was the principle victim of this chaos. An Alesian stomped on his bike and broke his back wheel. He was obliged to get Delattre to fix his bicycle.

The minds of those at Montpellier were already turned to the expected microcosm. The sporting contest on the road was beginning to become clearer. The leading group now contained no more than eight men: Maurice Garin, Aucouturier, Pothier, Cornet, Samson, Beaugendre, Catteau and Filly. These men came through at about 3:30 a.m. Garin drank the soup that Delattre had prepared for him. As for Pothier, he stuck to his own personal menu of peaches to start with and bread and cheese to finish. He began the race again with his mouth full. The road was waiting.

The day was breaking when the next group arrived six minutes down. It included: Cèsar Garin, Faure, Dortignacq, Chaput, Lombard and Jousselin. For the latter it was a triumph, but why? He was not a man from the area since he was born at Saintes, but the local journalists had sung his praises to such an extent that he had become the hero of the Col du Grand Bois, the one who had courageously faced up to his attackers. They did not know what bravery he had shown again at Nimes.

This 14th of July had meant that the celebrations started early. There was no shortage of people at the Place de la Comedie. The Golden Cock bar was overflowing. But more with red wine and lemonade than with beer. When there is so much aramon to be found locally, why go searching for barley and hops?

The crowd was much calmer at Bezier in the establishment which contained the fixed checkpoint. The aroma of coffee wafted through the area. Here, except for a few merrymakers, no one had stayed up late. They had gotten up early instead. And they had all come to the Avenue de Pezenas. The news had circulated and the incidents at Nimes were well known. The southern public took the news badly and felt guilty that people from their region had originated it. The ones who were most bothered observed that it was no way to thank *L'Auto* for having tried to entertain the population of the Midi region.

At 6:12 a.m., the register received proof of the presence of Maurice Garin, Pothier, Aucouturier, Cornet and Beaugendre. The little group had been reduced.

The "tough nuts," such as Garin, Pothier and Aucouturier seemed impregnable, but it was interesting to note that two other riders had joined them, Cornet, the little rider from Choisy-le-Roi, and Beaugendre, the inhabitant of Salbris, near Orleans. Filly and Catteau had paid the price of an acceleration by the star riders just before the town. They arrived, two minutes after the major quintet. Catteau was nervous. In reply to the question of what he wanted to eat, he replied, "Some eggs, some eggs!"

He swallowed five of them and began again like a madman, with Filly on his wheel.

The crowd had to wait half an hour for the arrival of Jousselin, then, much later, Cèsar Garin and Lombard. Then the worth of the rest of the riders was on display as usual, as the field stretched further and further. Certain competitors were appearing to be quite expansive and even comical. Dargassies, the "Blacksmith of Grisolles," needed no coaxing to say his piece. He claimed that next year he would arrange for an escort of gendarmes to protect him from the bandits of Saint-Etienne and the brutes from Ales.

There was no lack of spectacle. Sometimes it was dramatic. One rider, Prèvost, was nothing but bumps and bruises. This unfortunate man had crashed no fewer than eight times since Marseille.

Little by little the riders saw the shade of the plane trees shorten and finally disappear from the road. The heat had well and truly arrived. From now on their tongues were hanging out as they rode towards Narbonne. Now, as they could receive no sustenance from their team managers, they often stopped at the public fountains. Garin was content, for most of the time, to plunge his head into the water.

For the riders, the world consisted of two things only, the sun on their heads and the vines on either side of them. Grape vines as far as the eye could see. However, they gave nobody any ideas. Aucouturier, who at any other time loved his "plonk," did not feel that it was appropriate at the moment. In any other circumstances he would have gulped down a glassful or even the whole of the bottle which he carried in his handlebar bag. He said that it kept him going. In other events people had remarked that he seemed a little excited, and that his squint was more pronounced. For the moment, in this heat, "The Terrible" had chosen to remain sober. He had filled his bottle with licorice water.

At Narbonne, because of the early hour, there were few people on the streets. The confetti and spent firecrackers which were strewn about were evidence of the previous evening's festivities. As the clock on the Cafe de la Universe showed, at 7:17 a.m., five riders appeared. Cornet and Beaugendre had succeeded in staying in the company of the champions. But as it was a flying control the riders had to be content with just drinking. All the same Garin put a question to one of the controllers, "Have you had any news from the Buffalo?"

"The Buffalo?"

"Yes, from the Bol d'Or.."

"It seems that Georget and Petit-Breton are side by side with all the others far behind," Delattre's driver replied.

No comments from the riders, they had to get to Carcassonne.

The Bol d'Or always excited the crowds. It was an important traditional race disputed over a period of 24 hours, on the track and behind pacers. This year the pacers were riding tandems. In the past the method of pacing had varied a lot. At the beginning, in 1892, ordinary bicycles had to suffice, but in the following years there were tandems, then triplets and finally quadruplets, which were bicycles for four cyclists. It was necessary to go faster and faster. The rider had the ability to follow his pacers, it was up to them to force the pace. One day, in a similar type of race, a wind shield was even used. It was in London, in 1897. Two years later in Paris, as technology progressed, they were passed on to "motorized tandems." And the winner, the Englishman Wallers, covered more than 1,000 kilometers before the moon completed its journey around the earth.

In this year of 1904, it had been decided to revert to a simplified version of the race. The only form of shelter permitted to the riders was tandems, driven by muscle power. For the best of them, when the team showed signs of weakening, they were replaced by other men. For those who were not quite so good, they had fewer tandems at their disposal so they were left behind. Sometimes the unknown riders ran out of tandems completely and had to follow whatever wheel became available.

Maurice Garin was very interested in the Bol d'Or, not only because bicycle racing had been his profession for more than ten years, but also because this event was one of the top competitions in the cycling world. He knew Leon Georget well as he had already raced with him. But he was especially interested in a young man, of whom his brother Cèsar had spoken very well after having seen him at work in the Bordeaux-Paris race, Petit-Breton. This boy was only 22, but he showed a lot of promise. Absent from this Bol d'Or, another rider showed all the signs of being able to become a champion, Emile Georget, Leon's younger brother. Garin was not at all unhappy that these men were absent from the Tour. He also thought of another man who showed enormous promise, Louis Trousselier, author of some fine exploits over these same roads last year.

"Things will be a lot clearer this evening," he said to Pothier.

In fact, Pothier did not think a great deal about the Bol d'Or. The trackmen finished their event at 10:30 in the evening. The result would become known at 11 p.m. At that time he would be fast asleep. Already he felt dazed after such an eventful night. For the moment, he had to concentrate on following Aucouturier's wheel which was turning at a respectable speed.

He was nevertheless thinking of the 50F prime which was on offer at Carcassonne. It emanated from the president of a club, the Veloce Club of Preixan. This man must be very taken with the sport, not only did he give his time to the club, but he was prepared to open his purse as well.

Pothier arranged things with Garin. The latter would cleverly lead him out and allow him to take the prime. Even so he still had to fend off the crowd in order to achieve his object. A tight, compact crowd was pressing onto the road.

Happy with this lucrative operation, Pothier had other ideas in his head and said to Maurice, "Go to the end of the table to sign in. That is where the soup will be. Delattre will have it ready, you can always count on him."

It was true, someone was waving to him in the crowd, it was someone from La Francaise, "This way, another 50 meters!"

Being aware of the crush of spectators, he had preferred to situate his table further on. The two riders followed him. Beaugendre had leaned his bike against a tree while he signed the sheet. He had the greatest of difficulty in getting back to it. But now things were a complete shambles, so things were obviously quite difficult. It took the rider from Salbris a good two minutes to break clear from this crowd. During this time, Garin and Pothier had started to feed themselves.

But how were Aucouturier and Cornet faring? With this crowd it was very hard to spot them. One man however, had fixed his beady eye on them, Alibert, Aucouturier's manager. He was watching them closely. He took note of the fact that they were no longer together. Cornet had managed to quickly get clear of the fans. He had filled his pockets and had jumped on his bicycle. Alibert had seen all this and shouted to Aucouturier, "Quick! Go after him. You'll be able to catch him and then you've won!"

"The Terrible" understood. He pulled on the bars like a madman and quickly caught the Parisian. Garin and Pothier did not immediately realize what had happened, they could see little through such a dense crowd. Suddenly Garin went pale.

"What's happened to the others?"

Pothier did not reply, he was not looking at Garin, he was searching in the crowd. A young man with a straw hat on his head and who was interested in the fate of the two stars, came up to them.

"They went that way," he asserted, with his arm stretched out.

In his excitement, he rolled his 'r's more than any other villager from this county of the Aude River but the two riders understood. They jumped on their machines. On the road they were quickly joined by Beaugendre.

The others were already five minutes in front. From the top of the hill their pursuers could see them, emerging from a cloud of dust. The chasing trio shared the work. Garin did not appear to be at his best. His turns at the front were neither longer nor more vigorous than those of his two companions. They seemed to be riding without commitment.... As he turned around, Pothier could see Filly in the distance. This man was fighting like the devil himself. Since he had been dropped, just before Bezier, he had really ceded very little ground. At Carcassonne, he signed in only six minutes after Pother.

From his motorcar, Delattre cried out to his riders, "I'll go on ahead, I must keep an eye on Aucouturier."

So the two La Francaise riders were left to their own devices - a just compensation - to continue under the critical gaze of Alibert, "The Terrible's" manager.

At Castelnaudary, the country of the windmills, the correspondent of *L'Auto* had things ready. He had arranged a culinary surprise for Géo Lefèvre and his friends. It was a cassoulet, the real thing, a local cassoulet that was distinguished from a Toulouse cassoulet by the absence of sausages. He was going to look after these Parisians. And to be sure of doing so he had called on the services of the local expert. The riders should be arriving just before 12:15. Everything was planned, at 11:30 the staff of *L'Auto* would appear. They would promptly sit down at the table.

He pulled his watch out of his pocket: 10:45. A motorcar with banners could be distinguished just after, it was the *L'Auto* motorcar. For a moment the correspondent was confused before he received an explanation from Géo Lefèvre, "The riders are coming. They're just behind us."

A face froze, that of the man with the cassoulet who understood that he would not be able to honor his guests.

At 10:55, Aucouturier and Cornet signed in. Nine minutes later it was the turn of Garin, Pothier and Beaugendre. Their faces were scarlet. As they stopped the heat seemed to be overwhelming. On the road when turning the pedals it was better, moving through the air created a light breeze. Today the wind was blowing in the direction of the race, so the dust was less of a problem.

"We must get going," Géo Lefèvre said to the man with the cassoulet.

"There must be another occasion," replied the disappointed man. "Why not some time after tomorrow?"

"That's a promise, Castelnaudary's not far from Toulouse!"

A young rider arrived just after. A kid. He was 17 years old. It was Filly. A "good" rider who already knew his profession. His mother, in a moving letter, had written to *L'Auto* to ask them to look after him. She had not been able to hold him back, he wanted to go and play his part alongside the "greats," with Garin and Aucouturier. So it was that Abran,"the father of the outsiders," kept his eye on the youth at the stage finishes.

When another rider made his appearance, he was to receive a volley of whistles. It was Alfred Faure. At each checkpoint it was always the same. He was obviously associated with the hooligans of Saint-Etienne.

It was now only 58 kilometers to Toulouse. The pace of the two leaders was roughly the same as their followers, meaning that the time gap remained the same. Cornet was doing an enormous part of the work. Just to think that he only figured among the ranks of the "fourth category" before the start.

It was not yet one o'clock in the afternoon when the two leaders passed through the gates of Toulouse.

The town was in a turmoil. Twenty thousand spectators had streamed towards the Saint-Michel Avenue. The smooth-talking Abran had obtained everything he asked for. He received superb support from the man who had become his friend, Pons. Already, last year, he had played a major part in the success of the Tour's Toulousan welcome. A comment on Toulouse and its contribution to this Tour de France? Up to this point the staff gave the best demonstration of skill in organizing the stages and the intermediate check points as well as the ability to separate the athletes at the finish. Toulouse was to prove to be the yardstick by which all the other stage finishes were to be judged. For the moment everything was superbly ready. One single finishing line, to start with. And at the end of a long straight of 500 meters, protected by barriers, the road itself 10 meters wide, permitted everything to be "wrapped up" fairly. It was guarded by soldiers. All that remained for the riders to do was to demonstrate their sporting qualities. A large banner across the road indicated the precise spot where the stage finished.

As for the well-behaved public, there were stalls where coconut drinks and lemonade were available in large quantities. Next to them the officials of the municipality benefitted from a huge tent, decked out with flags, where they could frolic about at their ease. The conversations here varied from the jocular to the serious. But there was always the danger of politics rearing its ugly head! The Mayor said to Abran:

"Do not forget to come to the town hall tomorrow with Mr. Lefèvre and Mr. Pons."

"We'll come with pleasure," replied the great quartermaster.

An atmosphere of great excitement reigned in the area of the finishing line. The 14th of July must count for something. Red, white and blue flags were flying next to the banners above the heads of the crowd.

A trumpet rang out. Abran put down his glass and went out of the tent, with a steady pace and a well brushed moustache and beard, it just remained for him to straighten his hat.

The riders appeared. Although he was hardly interested in the sporting competition itself - which was not in the least any sort of paradox - Abran was surprised to see neither Garin nor Pothier.

At the end of a magnificent struggle, Aucouturier got the better of his young comrade. As he got off his bike, he was radiant and tried to put things in perspective. "You've seen this boy. He's called Cornet and I can tell you that he's more terrible than I am. He's eaten practically nothing all day and he has been terrific.

When he was leading, the pace went right up."

The little Cornet had to lower his eyes. He was only 20. He was a man from the rough side of Paris and was not used to being interviewed. "I cocked a snoot at the La Francaise riders. Next year I'll be riding to win!"

And Aucouturier added: "He's funny, this Cornet. Even during the race he finds the time to tell jokes. He plays the clown and is a wonderful mimic."

Cornet's cheerful nature was beginning to be noticed by everyone. Someone had said "He's a joker, this Cornet," and an accolade was made to the little man and his comic effects. Little by little he was called "The comic Cornet," or "Cornet the Comic." These titles were in no way critical and were no reflection on his capabilities. He might be a joker but he was a realistic one.

For the moment Alibert was deep in conversation with him. Perhaps the young rider was already a little in the Peugeot camp as he was riding a J.C. bicycle. In any case, he had been of great benefit to Aucouturier.

Another fanfare of trumpets. Roughly ten minutes had gone past. This time, it's Garin, Pothier and Beaugendre. They were classified in the reverse order. Garin finished with his hands on the top of his handlebars. Why do more? He was still at the top of the general classification.

Aucouturier wound up with another 400F in his pocket and improved his standing in the overall classification. Certainly he was still a long way behind the "Little Chimney Sweep." Obviously he regretted his dreadful first stage.

As far as they were concerned, Garin and Pothier seemed to be somewhat contrite at having let their two rivals escape. But they did have legitimate excuses. Pothier showed his bruised arm and the elder of the Garins explained that all day long he had been suffering from the effects of the blows he had received at Nimes. He nevertheless made it known that he felt as confident as ever.

"Providing that I am not assassinated before Paris, the Tour de France 1904 is mine in the same way as the 1903 one was!"

"Father" Maurice was well liked by the public. From the moment that he put his nose out of doors, he was recognized and acclaimed. His exploits had stayed engraved in most people's minds. But local pride always took first place. The townspeople were looking forward to seeing the two men from Toulouse, or at least they were certainly both residents of the Garonne, the inseparable Carrère and Dargassies.

As a consequence, the little Filly did not receive the amount of acclaim he deserved. This boy of seventeen finished sixth on the stage, only twenty-five minutes down on the leaders. Quite an exploit! In Touraine, at Loches, when his mother heard the news....

Carrère and Dargassies now arrived. Together! In the stands a man raised his arm, the leader of the orchestra. A vibrant rendition of "The Toulousain" rang out, and the crowd joined in with lusty voices. It was a moving moment which was to stay engraved in the memories of the two men who had provoked it. Another man arrived with them. But he understood that it would be wiser not to sprint, Alfred Faure. This moderation meant a more discreet arrival. He had no desire to be whistled at any more. The crowd demanded a lap of honor from Carrère and Dargassies. They accomplished this with delight, forgetting that they were as dusty as you could imagine. The beard of the "Blacksmith of Grisolles" seemed to be as powdered as an aristocrat's wig from the past. A supplementary and supreme honor was reserved for the two blue-eyed boys, the conductor of the orchestra led his men in a compelling "Marseillaise." And the public took up the anthem with fervor. Scarcely had this hommage finished when some rather strong men seized the two heroes and carried them away on their shoulders. If only Desgrange had seen that! What a superb Tour de France at Toulouse!

The newspaper boss was not entirely satisfied. And specifically not with the team that he had sent to the Tour. He had received letters of protest about the direction arrows on the crossroads which were unsatisfactory. It was the responsibility of Abran. He would be reprimanded! But Desgrange's discontent was especially directed towards Miral who had been supplying virtually no copy. Géo Lefèvre found a dispatch waiting for him at Toulouse: "Send Miral back to me quickly, he is useless." The poor Géo was very embarrassed to pass the order on to his companion, whose company he appreciated so much. He tried to console him.

"Don't be too upset, it's possible that cycling does not suit you too much, but you've made a good start in the fields of automobiles and aviation. That's where your future lies."

In fact, Jacques Miral's career was to later blossom when he became a commentator on these two motorized sports.

Abran did not yet know that he was about to be replaced as for the moment he was representing the boss at the Toulouse town hall. Because of his age and his imposing bearing, he had been charged with making a speech to thank the town counselors. To this end his speech was somewhat stereotypical. He use the words "thank you" more than ten times. Those who knew him found it rather amusing. After all, the mayor of Toulouse was not at Marseille and would not be at Bordeaux.

During the reception, next to the buffet, someone approached Abran and said, "In fact with your Tour de France, you are a little short!"

"Excuse me?"

"You have no stages of 1,500 kilometers!"

"Of 1,500 kilometers, have I heard you right, sir?"

"Perfectly. Do you know that our town is going to see the start of a Toulouse-Paris on foot, moreover organized by your newspaper, in a fortnight. 734 kilometers, sir, and on foot."

"Yes, that's right, I read that there are 20 starters. They are really going to suffer, the poor men. I would sooner be in my place than in theirs!"

Abran could not help thinking that it was all a little mad.

At their hotel, Garin and Pothier had received news of the Bol d'Or. It was the man from Nantes, Petit Breton, nicknamed "the Argentinian" because in his early youth he had followed his parents to Buenos Aires, who had won. With 852 kilometers, he had beaten the track record for the tandem-paced version, a record which had been held by Huret. The second-placed man, Leon Georget, had clocked up 810 kilometers, with the others much further behind. So it had really been a duel between two riders. Petit-Breton had not always been in the lead. At the tenth hour, Georget had overtaken him when his adversary had got off his bike to be massaged. This stop lasted for eight minutes during which time Georget had lapped the track several times. It took Petit-Breton a full four hours to regain the lead. Garin learned that the riders had suffered terribly in the heat. This did not surprise him, the bowl of the Buffalo track reflected the rays of the sun in a way that was hard to believe. All of the men had ridden in shorts, with bare legs. In the Tour the best riders preferred long tights, even in the Midi heat wave. Garin was amused to see that the Swiss Laeser, the same man who had started the Tour de France and retired on the first day after several setbacks, had finished in a fine fifth place in Paris.

The "Little Chimney Sweep" was quite satisfied with his position in the Tour de France. Had he not once again saved his bacon on the stage and kept his name at the top of the classification?

The results of Stage 3 - Marseille - Toulouse:

1. Aucouturier .... 15h 43 min 55 sec
      Bicycle - Peugeot
      Tires - Michelin
2. Cornet .... 15h 43 min 55 sec
3. Beaugendre .... 15h 52 min 8 sec
4. Pothier .... 15h 52 min 8 sec
5. Garin .... 15h 52 min 8 sec
6. Filly .... 16h 9 min 9 sec
7. Dortignacq .... 16h 26 min 2 sec
8 Catteau .... 16h 27 min
9. Garin, Cèsar .... 16h 35 min 52 sec
10. Jousselin .... 17h 14 min 52 sec
11. Dargassies .... 18h 00 min 40 sec
12. Carrère .... 18h 00 min 40 sec
13. Faure .... 18h 00 min 40 sec
14. Prèvost, Charles .... 18h 50 min 13 sec
15. Prèvost, Noel .... 19h 32 min 42 sec
16. Daumain .... 19h 49 min 56 sec
17. Driuol .... 20h 20 min
18. Samson .... 21h 2 min 44 sec
19. Gabory .... 21h 47 min 20 sec

Stage distance - 424 K (262.9 miles)
Winner's average speed - 28.80 kph (17.86 mph)

The general classification:

1. Garin, Maurice .... 48h 8 min 15 sec
2. Pothier .... 48h 8 min 38 sec

3.	Garin, Cèsar	49h 50 min 36 sec
4.	Aucouturier	50h 29 min 55 sec
5.	Cornet	50h 29 min 58 sec
6.	Beaugendre	50h 35 min 6 sec
7.	Dortignacq	52h 4 min 5 sec
8.	Faure	52h 19 min 42 sec
9.	Catteau	52h 51 min 5 sec
10.	Filly	53h 21 min 4 sec
11.	Jousselin	55h 43 min 52 sec
12.	Dargassies	56h 34 min 10 sec
13.	Gabory	57h 50 min 22 sec
14.	Prèvost, Ch	59h 50 min 19 sec
15.	Samson	61h 14 min 26 secs
16.	Maitron	61h 15 min 30 secs
17.	Carrère	63h 29 min 34 secs
18.	Paret	63h 29 min 34 secs
19.	Saget	64h 10 min 49 secs
20.	Chaput	64h 57 min 4 secs

Chapter 7
The Press Erupts

Unrest pursued this Tour de France and criticism followed in its wake. Desgrange reacted strongly. They wanted to bind him hand and foot to his rules, while these rules were designed simply to limit, if they could not entirely eliminate, the major excesses of the past. The coalition of badly understood regionalism and competition between the organs of the press, gave rise to a series of scathing attacks. It was in this way that some of them wholeheartedly supported the local riders while others published their extravagances.

Le Velo did not hesitate to fan the flames. It published the letter of a witness whose testimony must have been authorized as he was an "official controller."

"On Thursday, the 14th of July, riding in my 12 horsepower Motobloc motorcar and accompanied by Messrs. Dapot, chief consul of the U.V.F. and Badin, a consul, I followed, in my capacity as a controller, the Tour de France race between Carcassonne and Toulouse and was witness to certain events which forced me to lodge the following complaint:

"I the undersigned, Marius Leon Catinaud, supplied with the armband of an official controller of the annual Tour de France, certify to having seen between Carcassonne and Villepinte, rider A... No... followed and sustained by a motorcyclist dressed in town clothes of a dark grey color, a black leather cap, aged about 35 and by a cyclist wearing a brown woolen jersey, with a hat of the same color, blond, clean-shaven, both riding machines X...

"The rider A... No... accepted on two occasions, from the hands of the motorcyclist, drinks that the motorcyclist had prepared in advance. These facts constitute a flagrant infraction of the rules of the race. I believe that I am exercising my right and doing my duty by bringing them to your attention.

"Mr. Caubere, of *La Depeche* newspaper, riding in another motorcar and also a controller, witnessed the same events at the same time.

signed: M. Catinaud"

C. Badin

"I immediately sent this complaint to the organizers, but it was ignored.

"It is for this reason, sir, that I beg you to print my protest, leaving you free to comment on it as you see fit."

The letter A... of course referred to Aucouturier.

It remained for *Le Velo* to add its piece. The task was completed by Charles Ravaud, who ungraciously added, "Our comments will not be very long.

"We have already given sufficient examples to leave no one in doubt as to what we think of the decisions taken by the organizers of this priceless sporting event. Today the public is no longer deceived by trickery and knows perfectly well that the 1904 Tour de France constitutes the 'greatest sporting joke of the Century'.

"They had to reply to Messrs. Catinaud and Badin that they were 'troublemakers;' that you could not possibly immediately disqualify everyone, because a cyclist wearing a cap and light grey trousers insisted on preceding the riders and that when all was said and done the organizers had done everything in their power to ensure that the race was run in the most honest possible way.

"It is only fair to add that, they must say and repeat all these things in order to convince those who have been put on their guard that the Tour de France is not being run honestly."

Following this commentary, it is to be wondered how Charles Ravaud could possibly succeed in remaining on friendly terms with the two Georges, Abran and Lefèvre. But nevertheless he was later able to work with them on the staff of *L'Auto* without the least problem.

At the time, the acidity of the remarks were not lost on Géo Lefèvre. He too dipped his pen in hemlock.

"Poor old *Le Velo*, toothless, moribund and lamentable, has just slobbered out a pathetic criticism of our organizational skill.

"Its Bordeaux-Paris was run two months ago and it is public knowledge that there were so many frauds in the event that the U.V.F. has not yet been able to find a broom strong enough to entirely clear matters up. They have decided to draw attention away from themselves by taking it out on our Tour de France.

"It has published letters from the cities of Ales and Nimes, which to us seems natural enough, but it really exceeds the limits of stupidity, when it accuses both Aucouturier and Cornet of fraud without even bothering to check on the allegations, thus harming the reputation of two riders who will make it pay dearly for the harm it has done them."

Géo Lefèvre tried to support his remarks with a letter he had received from Beziers, it read, "Today, I read in certain local newspapers, and notably in *La Depeche*, an account of the Tour de France race.

"Mr. Jean Caubere, who signed his article in *La Depeche*, pretended to having seen, between Pazenas and Alzonne, a motorcar driving in front of the race, containing Aucouturier and Cornet.

"While recognizing Mr. Caubere's good sporting faith, I must in all truth say that he was making a grave mistake, and I believe that I was in a very good position to verify this, as it was I who was driving the motorcar in which Mr. Caubere believed he had seen Aucouturier and Cornet.

"Exactly what happened was this. After we saw Filly and Catteau pass through Carcassonne, we left them in order to catch the leading group. Around Pazenas we were very surprised to see that it no longer contained Aucouturier and Cornet. It was then that Garin said to us: 'Go in front and see if the others are up to something.'

"Immediately, we accelerated away and rejoined Aucouturier and Cornet who were some two kilometers in front and, contrary to what Garin, Pothier and Beaugendre thought, were riding as normally as possible, Cornet being in the lead with Aucouturier following. Moreover, it was absolutely impossible for them to be 'up to something', because there was a controller with them.

"We drew alongside Cornet and Aucouturier, and the latter asked us if they had a big lead on Garin and the others. After having informed them, we turned off, and it was at this moment that Mr. Caubere crossed in front of us and turned off the road another

20 meters further on. As he crossed in front of us again, Mr. Caubere waved to us and shouted out to us that the Garin group were behind them.

"At that moment, I left the riders and went straight to Bezier, after having followed the race for 125 kilometers.

"If my word is not enough, I can give you the names of four other sportsmen who were with me, and who are also ready to give their word of honor that during the whole time that we were able to see Aucouturier and Cornet, they had not been 'up to something' for a single second.

"Mr. Lautrec, your correspondent at Bezier, is also aware of these facts and would be able to confirm them.

"Be good enough to believe me, dear Sir, your totally devoted,

J. Pascal"

In spite of everything, the letter made no mention of the food that Aucouturier and Cornet were claimed to have received. Certainly the claim remained a strong possibility as when Pothier and Garin were taking on food at the control. Aucouturier and Cornet were on the road, furiously opening up a gap. But curiously, Delattre had lodged no protest. It seemed that the two teams, La Francaise and Peugeot had observed a "modus vivendi"[1] on the rule concerning feeding by a third party on the road; you could hardly reproach others for something that you practiced yourself. When all was said and done, taking account of subsequent cycling practices, it could hardly be regarded as cheating. On this point, the rules appeared to be somewhat archaic.

The local press reacted strongly, the incidents at Ales were difficult to stomach. And the people of Nimes continued to deplore them. *Le Journal du Midi*, located in the county town of Gard, echoed their sentiments. "Payan had been caught, four or five times, taking pace, against all rules. So it seemed that he deserved to be disqualified. But his fellow citizens had other ways of protesting instead of the ones they used. In no circumstances should they have attacked the riders who were in no way responsible. Their conduct was totally reprehensible.

"And if next year, in the wake of these incidents, the Tour de France does not come through here, the sportsmen of Nimes will be able to blame only themselves along with those of Ales."

L'Eclaire du Midi, whose offices were in Montpellier, came down on the side of the people of Ales, arguing that it was their duty to inform the public of the "downside and the intrigues of this so-called race of the Tour de France which had become no more than a hollow deception."

L'Auto was faced with an accusation that it was the La Francaise company which furnished the funds for the race and that it was agreed that one of their riders must win the event, no matter what the cost might be.

"A word of reply to this puerile idiocy will be enough. *L'Auto* is a limited public company and any shareholder has access to the details of the company expenditure. It will therefore be easy to see in one month's time who has paid for the prizes and who has paid for the race expenses."

Géo Lefèvre was battling against these accusations and this sourness when a rider, Alfred Faure, presented himself at the hotel. He gave him a letter and disappeared without revealing its contents. The journalist wasted no time in passing the gist on to his readers. "Faure came to give us a letter in which he said that he was retiring from the race in order to avoid being 'assassinated' before the end. It seemed to be a bit steep to me bearing in mind that he was visibly very tired and that, in spite of a certain amount of skill, he was in need of more training.

"And then, Faure being the instigator of the scandal at Saint-Etienne and by being in league with the assassins, did he then think that no one would hold him responsible for what happened? A piece of advice for the young, the very young Faure who has gained no sympathy whatsoever in our race, next year he must avoid all criticism of his comrades which caused sand to be thrown in their eyes, that he does not incite his friends at the control by claiming that everybody was united against him. These are the things that a man who finishes the race and wants to prove his worth cannot allow himself to do. Moreover, an unknown rider who was dropped on the first and on the third stages was probably in the leading group at Marseille mainly due to the fact that his rivals were discouraged by the assassins in the first-ever exhibition of hate in a public race and one which means that his town will be deprived of the Tour de France in 1905."

However, the fourth stage promised to be calmer for the simple reason that only 268 kilometers separated Toulouse from

Bordeaux and there was no need to ride during the night. Now as we have seen, it was the night, which cast its evil spell and which, under its cloak of darkness, the most somber plots were hiding.

The staff of *L'Auto* were busy with their own little stage. Do you know that they went to Castelnaudary to do honor to their host's cassoulet? As there were a dozen of them it needed a caravan of three motorcars to transport them. They were received with open arms by the local club. It can be confirmed that Georges Abran held his own at the table with Gaston Rivierre, the former devourer of kilometers.

---

1 "Modus vivendi" means "way of living".

Chapter 8
Toulouse-Bordeaux

They had arrived at Toulouse on Thursday at one o'clock in the afternoon and left again on Sunday at five o'clock in the morning. For the first time, the stage would be ridden totally in daylight. The distance would be shorter and the roads would be flatter. They would quite simply follow the course of the river Garonne, straying just once from the path when they went briefly to Montauban for a glimpse of the river Tarn.

Although it was possible to doubt some of them, these riders were all considered to be professionals, for the sole reason that the prizes were nailed to the top of the greasy pole and the covetous nature of these men urged them to climb it. This distinction permitted the organization to run, on the very same day, another "amateur" Toulouse-Bordeaux. Same distance, same route. People's minds were excited by the comparison. In order for things to be fair and so that no one could reproach the "greats" from taking pace from the "little ones," it was decided to start the amateurs half an hour later.

Before each stage, by virtue of the fact that cycling had adopted some of the traditions and practices of horse racing, the journalists gave their forecasts. If the jockey's silk blouse and cap (which were obligatory at the time of the penny-farthings) had been abandoned, many people did not hesitate from giving their prediction of the result even if there was no organized system of betting. Such conjecture was not delivered in the conditional tense, it was expressed with certainty, using the language of the clairvoyant. So the newspaper columns before the start of a stage could be divided into three parts: the schedule, the route, the forecasts. *Le Velo* and *L'Auto* always adhered to this framework. So Charles Ravaud was to write, "On a stage as short as this from Toulouse to Bordeaux (268 kilometers), you cannot count on Aucouturier, who will no doubt win the stage, and also expect him to significantly reduce some of his two hour deficit. The route is far too easy to permit such an exploit and the great Hippolyte will have to be content with snatching it from his rivals Pothier, Cornet, and the Garins in a sprint."

Henri Desgrange joined with him on all these points but with a few extra nuances. "So it is the great roadman Hippolyte Aucouturier whom I consider will be the winner of the Toulouse-Bordeaux stage; he will easily beat his adversaries by several lengths but I do not predict, apart from an accident, that this victory will significantly modify the general classification."

At about four o'clock, more or less awake, the riders were picking up their armbands in front of the Cafe Sion, the leading establishment in "la ville rose." Following that, they went in a procession to the Cafe Saint-Roche on the Avenue des Minimes. The reason for this double passage by way of these temples of lemonade was that each one of them made their own small contribution. It was in this sphere that Abran's preliminary work proved to be so useful. The Cafe Sion stayed open all night, resounding with an extraordinary activity. Spectators and consumers were able to admire their champions in the small hours of the morning. On seeing Garin, a lady, accompanied by a rather large gentleman, proclaimed, "My God, look how thin he is!"

"That is the minimum requirement, dear madam. In cycling you need muscles and bones. Did you not notice the liveliness in the eye of the champion?"

But the man who was surrounded more than anyone else, was sitting on a chair with his legs stretched out. It was Dargassies! He was in a somewhat hilarious mood. Behind his blond beard, the "Blacksmith" was thinking of 29 kilometers further on, he had an image of Grisolles, his village, where his supporters would greet him in triumph. These few days in his own area had done him an enormous amount of good, had he not been able to sleep in his own bed and had he not done a little work at his own forge?

The controller had taken note that Faure had announced that he would not be at the start. A nasty taste was removed from the Tour.

The amateurs as well, had already entered the lists. Abran would be able to drop his flag on both categories of riders. The big group of riders, professionals at the front, set off, followed by a large crowd. After a regrouping on the Avenue des Minimes, the starter liberated the professionals. They were obliged to slalom their way through the carts belonging to the peasants who had come to sell their wares at the Toulouse market. The amateurs still had 30 minutes to wait before setting off in their pursuit. There were 38 of them, almost all from the Bordeaux region.

Grisolles. Many cited the French proverb that it was by working at the forge that you became a blacksmith. The equivalent English expression is somewhat simpler if less colorful,"practice makes perfect." All the village was waiting for Dargassies. Some even had tears in their eyes. And he came through in the lead! What could be more natural for his peers than to allow him this pleasure. Just to think that later they would be reproached for this. Some people argued that as all the regionals passed through their own areas in the lead it was proof that the race was "fixed." But this was just one tiny part of the race. There was no lack of opportunity to go clear during the day, firstly by their respective strength but also by the hard roads which sapped their strength. The bikes were all excellent - do not imagine that they were like carts - they were well made and comfortable to ride, their tires exuded quality. It was only the roads which revealed their weaknesses. We have mentioned it very little, but only the other day, just outside Beziers, the riders were beginning to wonder if they would ever survive the holes they kept riding into in the middle of the night.

At the exit from Grisolles, ruthless measure had been taken. Nails were everywhere on the road. One man swore. Dargassies. Just to think, in his home town! But his cry had hardly been heard. Aucouturier, another victim, shouted out as well. An onlooker had immediately given him a bicycle but, it was doubtlessly inferior compared to his fine Peugeot which he had been riding a few moments before. He restarted but, naturally, had lost ground. It was nothing to speak of but then: ppfff! he had picked up another shiny point.

"Murderers!" he screamed.

He was given a third machine. What happened then? He punctured a third time, under the doleful eye of Géo Lefèvre. It could be stated that his disappointment was as sharp as the point of the nail that pierced his tire. With no help in sight, he rode on the rim. It was not before he had covered ten kilometers in this fashion that he met his saviour, a sergeant-major mounted on a very fine machine. But he had to persuade the soldier to hand it over. However, the negotiations did not last too long. So there he was charging along at 40 kph in the pursuit of his rivals. All along the road he passed unfortunate riders who were bewailing their luck alongside their bicycles with flat tires.

The others were approaching Montauban, 51 kilometers after the start. The first fixed control was waiting for them there. The five sporting clubs of the town had been mobilized so the road was under close scrutiny. The leader went through at 6:32. They had not been taking it easy. A timekeeper revealed that the first amateurs had taken six minutes longer than the leading pros.

Thirty kilometers further on, at Moissac, at the flying control, it was possible to take stock of the situation. The leaders were: the Garin brothers, Pothier, Carrère, Jousselin, Beaugendre, Daumain and Maitron. They had maintained an average speed of above 33 kph for 81 kilometers. Aucouturier followed them at two minutes; he had considerably reduced his deficit.

He was preparing to join the leaders at the end of an exceptional pursuit, when he punctured again. And both tires at once! L'Auto's motorcar stopped alongside him. Would the occupants be content just to sit and watch him? Once again he had to repair it alone. He was half way through the operation when Cornet arrived. He too had been a puncture victim. He waited for his companion. This was not the time for him to tell his jokes, as the great Hippolyte was boiling with rage! They began again together. But Cornet picked up another nail and had to let Aucouturier disappear into the distance.

Agen. Each fixed control gave rise to a real bicycle festival. All that the region contained in the way of enthusiasts rushed to be there. And Agen was one of the most important cycling towns of the past, along with Bordeaux, Angers and Saint-Etienne. There were just a handful of men who were responsible for this situation. Here the catalyst was Dr. Georges Thomas. He presided over the destiny of the Union Velocipedique de France for four years, from

1889 to 1892, in the days when the bicycle finally supplanted the penny-farthing and cycling really established itself. Today, he was present, first of all to donate a prime but also to help to operate the control.

The county of Lot-et-Garonne, had always inspired cyclists, from the beginning. It was in this place that one of the very first historians of the bicycle and cycle sport, Louis Bonneville, was born, in Villeneuve-sur-Lot. At the control he was to be seen everywhere, smiling as he helped everyone just as he had already done at Toulouse.

In this way as well, an unknown man from Castillones who was however, the first "recordman" of the Tour de France by bike. He was called Joyeux. Theophile Joyeux. And his triumph went back to ... 1895. The fact appeared to be so astonishing - for as far as it was known the Tour de France was created in 1903 at the initiative of Henri Desgrange and of Géo Lefèvre - but we must stop ourselves here, at Agen, in order to fully appreciate this fascinating past.

Theophile Joyeux's expression will never leave us. The man was in the corner of the Cafe Foy. Nobody notices him. He had ridden his bike 60 kilometers in order to see his "successors." And the Tour de France remains in him. However, as Joyeux admits, he was not the first to have the idea. This belonged to Jean Corre, a Breton and former rival of Charles Terront, the archetype of the French cycling champion. Corre had acquired a certain amount of notoriety due to his taste for long distance events. It was at the end of April, 1895 that he let it be known that he would establish the "record" for the Tour de France. At this time, the successful attempts over such and such a route or over such and such a distance were called records. Even if there were no antecedents. The date of the start was established, printed and then distributed to the press for publicity reasons.

But before then, he had to undergo one last test, a rather demanding exercise as it meant riding the Bordeaux-Paris. He put his name down in the roadman category and... finished first. In the classification which comprised the sprinters, the roadmen and the amateurs, he took fourth place. This exhausting race which took as much out of the body by way of preparation as it did by competing in it, had perhaps taken the edge off his form. In any case he felt obliged to postpone his start of the "big loop."

So Corre was quite shocked when he learned that another rider, Joyeux to be exact, was going to attempt the record of a Tour of France of which the distance would be 4,500 kilometers. Corre himself, had planned to do 5,000 kilometers, but this reduced distance was less important; he would not be the first to hold the record. Imagine his anger.

His objections appeared in the pages of the sporting journals. "It's not possible. Joyeux cannot do this to me, he cannot start before me. It's me who thought up the idea. The Tour de France belongs to me!"

And, he added strongly, "It's piracy!"

So Joyeux tried to physically initiate the story of the Tour de France. He too, was a professional but not one of great repute and his performances never matched those of the Breton from Plestin-les-Greves. The two men had already met each other in several races. During the history of the first Paris-Brest-Paris, Joyeux finished eighth, some way behind Corre, who was fourth. The following year, in the heroic Paris-Clermont Ferrand, known as the Michelin race, because the organizers had thrown nails on the road in order to demonstrate the ease with which their tires could be repaired, he took thirteenth place. It was only later, in 1893, that he established himself, going as far as to challenge Corre in a long and exacting event. For the first time, he put himself up against the Breton. Sure of himself, he did not hesitate to snub his adversary.

"Since my challenge to Corre appeared in Le Velo, Corre has shown no sign of life. Is he dead? Or is it that the 1,000 kilometer champion of the road is afraid to race without a pacer; does the distance frighten him?"

He descended to the language of a street trader. "If Corre believes that I am bragging when I offer to race against him over 2,000 kilometers, on the road or on the track, if he thinks he is mistaken, I say again 2,000 kilometers on the road or on the track..."

As could be seen, relations between the two men were not entirely cordial. Unless, of course it was all just one big publicity stunt!

Bordeaux-Paris, which Corre should have made light of, was run on the tenth of May, 1895. Joyeux was to start on the 11th, before the Breton had had time to recover, so cutting the ground from under his feet. His program comprised of 18 days, which was somewhat ambitious.

100

Early in the morning he left the gates of Paris by the Porte Maillot, full of confidence. He did not have long to wait for his first setback. Right from the beginning he came up against the most appalling weather conditions. This had an adverse effect on his schedule. Waterlogged by the rain, there was little news of his epic ride over the first few days. Joyeux's trail was picked up again at Arles, on the eighteenth of May in the evening. It was noted that he was riding around France in a clockwise direction. His route continued by way of Montpellier and Bezier and his passage was certified by the dispatches of the controllers. At Narbonne, one of them noted that, "Joyeux, arrived, went to bed at Narbonne. The Acetene bicycle is still marvelous and greatly admired by all." It was to be understood that the candidate for the record was subsidized by a make of bicycle which produced a machine which was out of the ordinary, it had no chain, but the effort of pedaling was transmitted to the back wheel by a shaft and bevel. His Metropole Acetene bicycle had been on the test bench for some time and benefited from all the publicity. The magazine *Le Cycle* published an article singing the praises of the machine. Joyeux, in the middle of his adventure is said to have written to his wife, "Sell my bicycle at home. I am going to keep the Acetene which I'm riding. I think it's wonderful and do not want to ride anything else."

This type of bike reached the peak of its glory thanks to Gaston Rivierre. It was with this model that our present motorcyclist won his three Bordeaux-Paris.

The benefits of the publicity that Joyeux drew on to himself were not solely to the profit of his machine. Joyeux was also under contract to a tire manufacturer and he did not hesitate to indicate the confidence he had in his tires, "although at this time of the year, he had to contend with the curse of newly graveled roads." It confirmed the quality of the G J tires!

In spite of the soaked highways which were hidden from his wheels, Joyeux continued his long trip. But obviously bad weather delayed him. So much so that between Quimper and Morlaix, the journey took 36 hours longer than expected. The barometer showed signs of improvement, which helped him to believe that he would be able to make up for lost time.

And the forecasters were right. On the 30th of May the "buckle was buckled," Joyeux entered into Paris by the Porte Maillot.

Just like every cyclist with any sporting pretensions, he rode his bike to the Cafe de l'Experance, the end-of-the-Century establishment which was so valued by the pedaling enthusiasists. Then he fulfilled one of his greatest needs by going to clean himself up. After an hour had elapsed, he reappeared with a calm expression, a flower in his buttonhole and a smile on his lips. He would now be able to take part in a magnificent lunch given in his honor.

He was so fresh, that apart from a sunburnt face, you could never have picked him out from the guests as the one who had completed the very first "Tour de France."

Why was it that the specialized press spoke of 5,500 kilometers instead of the 4,500 which he actually covered? We will never know. As is so often the case with someone achieving a particularly outstanding performance, objections were raised. By Jean Corre of course. He used the columns of the *Veloce-Sport* to argue his case.

"Before trying to beat the record of the Tour de France established by Joyeux, I meticulously checked the itinerary which had been adhered to. The result was that I established that Joyeux should have covered only 4,429 kilometers and not the 5,500 that was published. The difference of 1,071 kilometers appeared to me important enough to be taken into account when evaluating the worth of the performance..."

In Joyeux's defense, it must be said that when his attempt was announced, the distance of 4,500 kilometers was certainly mentioned. But the sensationalists took a hand, as much among the journalists as among the industrialists and financiers of the cycling industry. Our recordholder took no account of this, declaring that Corre had only to start on the date that he had announced in order to struggle against the same bad weather conditions. He thought that such a situation would help to establish which of them was the better. And, he added, "If Corre starts, as I want him to, and beats my record, as he hopes to, I will beat his time, that is the only challenge that I will accept from him."

So the ball was now in Corre's court. The man who thought up the whole idea of the Tour de France was obliged to put off his start several times. He was not available before September, while his route had been printed and sent to the press along with some of the regional clubs, in May. His trek covered a total of 5,012 kilometers. Unlike that of Joyeux, it was known to all. Every town that he passed through could be pinpointed.

Corre wanted to pull off something special. Nineteen days on the road was one less than Joyeux, but with 550 extra kilometers. His daily average would be 250 kilometers. He was assured of the help of some advertisers, and as far as equipment was concerned, he had some innovations which were very surprising for 1895. But were they not somewhat... utopian?

"Corre will not have to spend his time repairing or pumping up his tires, he is using ones with self-sealing inner tubes, of the Larue brand. He is so sure of the advantages of them that he laughs at the prospect of having a puncture and will not even be carrying a pump."

So when he started, on the 12th of September, also from the Porte Maillot, a lot of cyclists had fitted their bicycles with these inner tubes, and amused the onlookers by driving scissors and pins into them. There was another publicity stunt, after he returned, singing the praises of a bike made of aluminium and weighing only 8.5 kgs, that he was supposed to have ridden. But there was no proof that he had ridden it over the entire length of the course. In all probability he rode a machine made of steel weighing around 12 kgs, which, according to Veloce-Sport, was the average weight of the racing bikes used in that year's Bordeaux-Paris.

As a professional, Corre knew the importance of using first-class equipment and seasoned pacers. From the start he called on the assistance of one cyclist and two tandemists. Although hampered by a strong headwind, he rode a fine first stage, Paris-Rouen-Le Havre-Dieppe, a distance of 321 kilometers. The procession of helpers presented a somewhat comical picture. One of his pacers carried a bag over his shoulder containing a large loaf of bread, ready to be fed to Corre if he called for it.

Although the event took place at the end of September, Corre, unlike Joyeux, was confronted with hot weather. He quickly reduced his schedule during the second stage, to stop at Calais after only 200 kilometers. After passing through Lille and Valenciennes, he was seen approaching Sedan where a fine welcome was waiting for him. All the cyclists of the town had come to meet him and they all applauded him. At the end of the fourth day, he had ridden 907 kilometers. But he was already eight hours down on his timetable.

On the sixth day, he was seen at Pontarlier, after having ridden 1,468 kilometers. He then started to make better progress. The

Alps, which figured on his schedule between Grenoble and Nice, by way of the Sisteron, reduced his daily average, even if he did not ride over the high passes. When he stopped at Marseille, after 2,375 kilometers, he was running two days late. The next day, at Bezier, he was greeted by a large crowd, which helped him to reach his stop at Narbonne. For several days he had been affected as much by the intense heat as he had been by the poor condition of the roads. On the other hand, he appreciated the presence of local riders and the way they paced him. Often these were some of the best riders in the area.

His deficit increased and he was now three days down. *La Bicyclette* claimed that it was due to a temporary illness but there was no evidence of this. The *Veloce-Sport*, noting that the level of his performance was going down, now spoke of a "journey" around France. After a large incursion into the Southwest by way of Pau, Bayonne, Bordeaux and La Rochelle, he reached Saint-Nazaire. Curiosity and sympathy waited him everywhere, up to the point where at this halt the representatives of the press brought out the champagne in his honor.

Further on, he became a little more apathetic, no doubt because he did not appreciate the hilly country in Brittany and Normandy. Laboriously putting Brest, Saint-Brieuc, Cherbourg, Caen, Evreux and Mantes behind him, he finished this Tour de France in a flood of rain. At the Porte Maillot it was noted that he had lost some weight, which was compensated by his sunburnt face. It took him twenty five days to cover the 5,000 kilometers. His daily average had been 200 kilometers. Joyeux had been credited with 225 kilometers a day.

Even for 1895, neither of them could claim to have produced an outstanding performance. In the same year, the Englishman Mills rode the 1,400 kilometers which separated the south of England from the north of Scotland in three days and five hours. The weather was certainly worse than Corre had experienced, which was eighteen days of heat followed by torrential rain. It was hardly conducive to producing a great performance, but he had realized his idea of a Tour de France which was to be the forerunner of the great competition which we know today.

But Joyeux could say, "I was the first."

For the moment, he had come to welcome Garin who he had practically seen start on his career, more than ten years before. He spent some time at this control at Agen. The control sheet showed that some damage had been done. If the Garin brothers, Pothier, Beaugendre, Jousselin and Carrère came through the "nailed sections" unscathed, Aucouturier only appeared a quarter of an hour later with Cornet at half an hour. One of the lesser-known riders arrived on foot, and restarted on a hired machine. The procession continued for another six hours, with the pros mixed up with the amateurs.

At Marmande, the town known for its tomatoes but also for the popular sprinter Bourrillon, the crowd was enormous. The riders arrived there in the full heat of the day. The positions remained unchanged, the leading group had maintained half an hour's lead over Aucouturier and Cornet, who were now riding together. All of the roadmen flung themselves at the drinks. Garin, very sure of himself, advised his companions, "Don't forget to eat, there's still 86 kilometers to go!"

He himself swallowed some broth and some eggs. During this time, Delattre slipped a small bottle of lemonade into the bag on his handlebars.

"Father" Maurice was not unhappy to know that Aucouturier and Cornet were behind. It was revenge for the other day. However, it was a little puzzling. Would it ever be known if his group had ridden over the same sharp points as his followers? To put it plainly, did not the nails appear only after the first riders passed through? It hardly seemed likely that the mischief occurred only behind Garin and his group.

The check points always showed the weaknesses of the lesser riders. They arrived suffering, glassy-eyed and looking a little feverish. When Garin advised Carrère to consume some food, he replied that he was only thirsty and did not feel like eating. Like his colleagues, he plunged his head into a bucket of cold water put at his disposal, then asked for something to drink. Géo Lefèvre held out a bottle of lemonade to him which he greedily swallowed. His face was streaming with sweat; he had produced a tremendous effort just to stay with the riders who were clearly much better than he. His chest was heaving. He sat down. It was at that precise moment that the others left. Just the same he did eat a juicy peach, then he returned to the road, weighed down with a bottle of lemonade.

After a few kilometers, he had already emptied the contents.

Géo Lefèvre then saw him stop in front of a farm and ask for something to drink. He was never to rejoin his companions again as he hauled his suffering body to the finish. In 80 kilometers he was to lose two hours.

The countryside heat was torrid. If the incessant valleys offered an attractive picture to the riders, it was fortunate that there were no climbs to speak of as the road undulated among the hills as easily as the River Garonne did. Even so the route was not entirely lifeless, there were motorcars to be seen, sputtering and smoking, but above all there were farm carts everywhere as it was harvest time. Heavy carts pulled by impressive looking horses and sometimes obstructing the riders' way. Each time the cyclists, already surrounded by dust, were obliged to penetrate an even thicker cloud. Would they surface these roads one day?

Ouzou and Lefèvre were satisfied. Whenever they stopped they could quickly catch up with the riders. Their Cotterreau automobile could do 70 kph. Their dress for the day was rather amusing. Enormous floppy hats came down to their shoulders. The sun would not be able to overheat their brains!

Up until this time, two other unrated riders accompanied the trio of La Francaise leaders, Beaugendre and Jousselin. The latter, a big strapping fellow, was adapting well to this route which was designed for the strong men. He was dropped from the group after a puncture. So at Langon, at the flying control, there were no more than four of them still with a hope of contesting the stage victory. So Beaugendre was doing the ride of his life. He even did his turn at the front. The quartet was riding perfectly together. But these men were being tortured by an unquenchable thirst. When a fountain came into sight, they stopped as one man. Then set off again at top speed. This lack of facilities on the road was greatly to affect the average speeds.

The scenery changed again. They were now in the vineyards. Two types of grapes could be distinguished, most of them were dark green but others were almost white. The leaves next to the road disappeared under a fine dust.

They soon reached Langon. It was the last flying control before the finish. The riders did not have to stop. But, in this heat a little trip to the waiting water buckets was essential. It had to be done quickly. A customer cried out to Beaugendre, who was not close to the others, "Do you want my glass?"

"Why not? Thank you my friend!"

And the rider from Salbris swallowed the lemonade. He emitted a gassy belch as he put the glass down.

"Thank you, that was very good, nice and sweet."

The man gave him another glass. Beaugendre was not going to refuse it. Suddenly his face froze and he went red as he turned his head and vigorously demanded to know the young Garin's whereabouts.

"Where's the second Garin?"

He did not even wait for a reply, he understood - Cèsar had taken off. No doubt with the approval of his elder brother and of Pothier.

Beaugendre jumped back on his machine with anger in his soul. The escapee was some way away, he could not even see him. Garin Junior already had a lead of two kilometers. He was riding incredibly fast.

Maurice Garin and Lucien Pothier sat on the wheel of the rider from Loir-et-Cher. It was up to him to do the chasing!

Was the race won for the young Garin? This would be to ignore fate. The pothole could not have been very large. You could not hear the air escaping. The younger Garin stopped and pumped up his tire furiously. With an anguished look he called Géo Lefèvre who had just gotten out of the Cotterreau, "Where are the others?"

"One or two kilometers behind, no more."

He began again at the same frenzied pace. He kept one eye on his tire. But the inevitable happened, ten kilometers later, when he was pumping up his tire again, the others caught him. He was able to stay with them. It was the fountains that saved him. Beaugendre wanted to stop at most of them, and each time he did Cèsar used the opportunity to replace some of the air which had escaped from his tire. This was Bouscat. More pumping. He was safe, the finishing control was only another five kilometers at Pont-de-la-Maye.

Géo Lefèvre had already arrived there. He warned them of the imminent arrival of the leaders. A finish similar to the one at Marseille was planned. First a finish duly timed and recorded, then a neutralized section of seven kilometers leading to the Park Velodrome where the riders could start again. The public would be able to benefit from the spectacle of these courageous roadmen.

At Pont-de-la-Maye the crowds were dense in front of the Cafe Au Petit Trianon. It had been decked out with dozens of red, white and blue flags which were now flying in the wind. *L'Auto* had used the first floor to attach its big banner which marked the finish. Posters calling on the public were pasted to the walls and the nearby fencing. Some spectators had come on the tram whose rails went right past the cafe, but most preferred to use their bicycles. Standing there, holding their machines they were awaiting the arrival of their heroes. Life still went on as normal. There was a peasant wearing a beret crossing the road pulling a calf by its ear. A dog barked after the animal. No one was surprised, everyone was familiar with country life.

Suddenly, the cloud of dust, which had stayed with the riders since they left Toulouse, appeared. You could believe that it was this cloud that transported this little world along and then put it down where it wanted to. Four riders could be made out. Were they going to try to separate themselves and then glean one or two seconds during the race at the velodrome? No, they passed Abran and the timekeepers in one compact little group. The great quartermaster, after officiating at the dawn start at Toulouse, kept to his evening contract for the operations at the finish. The "great smoking brother" had not let him down. The railway was very good indeed.

Cèsar Garin was given another bicycle, a clean one with pumped up tires. The quartet, with papers certifying their arrival time in their pockets, went towards the race track in the park.

Numerous seats were already occupied. But the riders had not kept to their expected schedule. It was only two o'clock in the afternoon and they were expected to arrive later. So not everyone saw the battle between the first-placed riders. They had completed their 268 kilometers at an average speed of almost 31 kilometers an hour!

The four heroes lined up. They had to ride three laps of the track. When the bell range for the last lap, their speed was not very high. Pothier went to the front but, on the last bend the quartet came back together again. A final bust by Pothier and he took it in front of Cèsar and Beaugendre while Maurice had not even tried to get past them. The 350F prize went to the "Butcher of Sens," less money than on the previous stages.

Just after, Jousselin rode his three laps and then it was the turn of Aucouturier and Cornet. These two put on a fine display of speed. Aucouturier was just able to nip the Parisian. He was credited with the fine time of one minute and twenty seconds.

The day proved to be an immensely popular success for the organization of *L'Auto*. Géo Lefèvre took advantage of the opportunity to say:

"I saw more than ten thousand peasants looking at their copies of *L'Auto* in the fields today. That's enough to prove that the Tour De France is certainly the finest sporting invention of the Century."

And where were the amateur riders in all this? The first of them finished one hour and forty-three minutes behind the professional quartet. If the classifications had been mixed in together, he would have finished the stage in 13th place. Congratulations to Dias who largely dominated all his adversaries.

So only two riders paid the price of this day which bristled with "nail sections," Aucouturier and Cornet. The classification showed that it was just the two of them who had lost time.

These are the results of stage 4 - Toulouse - Bourdeaux:

1. Pothier	8h 40 min	6 secs
2. Garin, Cèsar	8h 40 min	6 secs
3. Beaugendre	8h 40 min	6 secs
4. Garin, Maurice	8h 40 min	6 secs
5. Jousselin	8h 50 min	2 secs
6. Aucouturier	9h 11 min	5 secs
7. Cornet	9h 11 min	5 secs
8. Maitron	9h 20 min	30 secs
9. Catteau	9h 30 min	15 secs
10. Gabory	9h 48 min	20 secs
11. Dortignacq	10h	
12. Dargassies	10h 11 min	15 secs
13. Carrère	10h 49 min	
14. Filly	11h 26 min	2 secs
15. Chaput	11h 30 min	
16. Daumain	11h 30 min	
17. Grimenwald	11h 30 min	
18. Rist	11h 30 min	
19. Colas	11h 40 min	30 secs

20. Samson .... 11h 59 min

Stage distance: 268 K (166.16 miles)
Winner's average speed: 30.95 kph (19.19 mph)
General Classification:

 1. Garin, Maurice .... 56h 48 min 22 secs
 2. Pothier .... 56h 48 min 44 secs
 3. Garin, Cèsar .... 58h 36 min 43 secs
 4. Beaugendre .... 59h 15 min 13 secs
 5. Aucouturier .... 59h 41 min
 6. Cornet .... 59h 41 min 4 secs
 7. Dortignacq .... 62h 4 min 4 secs
 8. Catteau .... 63h 21 min 20 secs
 9. Jousselin .... 64h 39 min 34 secs
10. Filly .... 66h 47 min 6 secs
11. Dargassies .... 66h 48 min 25 secs
12. Gabory .... 67h 38 min 42 secs
13. Maitron .... 70h 36 min
14. Carrère .... 73h 10 min 40 secs
15. Chaput .... 76h 27 min 4 secs

Chapter 9
Bordeaux-Nantes

To an extent we have glossed over this fourth stage, as if the affair with the nails appeared to be of little consequence compared to the events at the Col du Grand Bois and at Nimes. It was felt that things had already been decided and that Aucouturier, strong as he was, would not be able to gain back three hours on Garin and Pothier.

They had arrived on a Sunday early in the afternoon. They would restart on a Wednesday at ten o'clock in the evening. Racing in the dark was different. Would the night reveal more skulduggery?

The little game of forecasting, which kept the reader in suspense, began anew. Charles Ravaud in *Le Velo* estimated that Aucouturier, although the best of them all, seemed to be dogged by bad luck, and that as a consequence, the stage would go to Maurice Garin. Henri Desgrange for *L'Auto* said that such misfortune could not last forever and that, as no rider came up to Aucouturier's standard, it was he who would win at Nantes.

Sunday's "little jaunt" was mainly forgotten by the Wednesday when the riders assembled on the north side of Bordeaux, at the well-known landmark of the Four Pavillions. This very same spot had seen the start of the first Bordeaux-Paris in 1891. It was the meeting place for a lot of people, commencing with those engaged in the Tour, former participants of the "Derby,"[1] but also the entourage of the moment, Rivierre and Jiel-Laval. The latter was appearing for the first time on this Tour de France. He was the most glorious of all the Bordeaux cyclists, the instigator of the initial Bordeaux-Paris, where he took fifth place behind the untouchable Englishmen. Today, it was on four wheels that he made his appearance, to watch over the first half of the stage.

The elegant Monsieur Abran was not missing at the rendezvous. Once again, he had been working hard during the stop at Bordeaux. He had been seen fussing over his "isoles"[2] but also doing his duty by being present at the banquet organized in honor of the representatives of *L'Auto* by the Burdigala, the club of the man who won the amateur Toulouse-Bordeaux. Once again, he made a speech. Once again, those who had been accompanying him noticed how similar it was to previous ones. Was he using carbon paper?

It had been noticed at the Four Pavillions that the daytime temperature had been much lower, a reassuring sign for those who did not enjoy being roasted by the sun.

The U.V.F. had taken charge of things. Mr. Pujo, its chief-consul, a term which pompously identified him as the regional delegate, was officiating with a somewhat overbearing manner. Jiel-Laval, who had been the previous holder of the post, accompanied him step by step. He had just come out of his hat and glove shop, an elegant and prosperous establishment which he had won by the sweat of his brow on the road. Another personality was not far away, Maurice Martin, one of the "fathers" of Bordeaux cycling and a journalist for the *Petite Gironde*. He too, had made sure to be at the start. It was he who, each year since its very inception, had started the riders on their trip from Bordeaux to Paris. The riders were surrounded by the many race followers. They all appeared to be more elegantly dressed than normal. Why was this? Simply because they had all been given new armbands. *L'Auto* thought they were well deserved as the sun and the dust had made the old ones unrecognizable.

Louis Bonneville, who had joined the organization at Toulouse, drove the second official race car.

But what was the main news of the day? Henri Desgrange arrived. He was to follow the stage on board a motorcar, a Motobloc. It had been put at his disposal by the director of this Bordeaux manufacturer. The number of makes of cars on the market was quite surprising even if the concept of motoring had not been fully developed. Faced with this overabundance, Henri Desgrange had to win the favor of all of them. The title of his newspaper reminded him of his function in the world of motoring.

He had just been designated as one of the administrators in the next motor show in Paris and as a member of the committee of the International Exhibition of Liege, planned for the next year.

Desgrange had come incognito. No rider, no team manager knew of his presence. He was there to surprise those who failed to adhere to the rules of their strict moral code. He would castigate those who strayed from the regulations. He would surprise the nail throwers and stop all kinds of cheating. In order to do that, he had laid his plans like a private detective. He had settled on a chauffeur's uniform. Already hidden behind a large windscreen, under a large cap, he concealed his gaze behind the driver's goggles. Here he was emerging from the shadow of a tree and saying, as he reached the motorcar, that he would wait for the riders at Libourne.

When the riders were called, two of them did not answer. Tachet, who up to this point had been rather discrete, and Beaugendre, the third-placed man at Bordeaux. Concerning the latter, many had the feeling that some sort of controversy was in the air. He claimed to have been obstructed in the sprint by the Garin brothers but the officials had not upheld his claim. The temperature had risen and his manager had advised him to retire from the race in order to demonstrate his discontent. This is what he did, but when all was said and done, it was he who was penalized, being robbed of the last two stages.

It did not prevent 33 riders from disappearing into the twilight at precisely ten o'clock p.m.

There were no more than 20 of them at Libourne, under the inquisitive gaze of Desgrange. Of course all of the best of them were among the number. At Barbezieux, in the middle of the night, 92 kilometers after the start, the leading group had been reduced to 15, following the usual pattern. To the people manning the flying control, a rider shouted for help, "Water, give me some water!"

"Are you thirsty?" someone replied.

"No, it's for my acetylene lamp, I need water for it."

The "isoles" really needed some sort of illumination. The water which dripped onto the carbide of their lamp helped them to do just this, by liberating the gas which supplied the required light. It was not as good as the headlights of the motorcars which were following the leaders, but it helped them to avoid a few of the potholes.

After the exit of from Barbezieux, where the sky was pitch

black, they took the road to Pons. According to the organizers there was no question of going to Cognac by the direct route. All of those who saw their tires give up the ghost on this rough secondary road could only deplore the choice.

Slowly, while they were heading east, a red glow could be seen on the horizon. Daybreak, at last!

At Cognac, the hustle and bustle of the fixed control. They had gone past the 150 kilometer point. Desgrange had not abandoned the leading group since Libourne. Had he seen any scheming? Some fraudulent move? No, not the slightest thing up until this point. He removed his disguise and greeted the local officials. The Cafe du Louvre, given the task of welcoming the race, was filled to overflowing. Outside, several thousand people had not been put off by the early hour from coming to see the giants of the road. And among the riders, there was an authentic giant, Jousselin, noticeable because he was at the head of his comrades. Now this man was from Saintes and so a Charentais through and through. It was he who they had come to see. His odysseys of the Col du Grand Bois and of Nimes, where he had been forced to fight, were known to all.

Jousselin arrived first. What luck! He went immediately to sign in under the cheers of his compatriots. By his side, the two Garins, Pothier, Aucouturier, Cornet,Samson, Gabory, Dortignac, Maitron, Daumain and Charles Prèvost. Once again it was noticed that those second-raters who had avoided puncturing had succeeded in staying with the leaders. Other men, such as the young Filly and also Catteau, Carrère and Dargassies had fallen afoul of the poor road surface, although none of them had picked up any nails.

The welcome at Cognac was nothing for Jousselin, compared with what had been prepared for him at his home town of Saintes. When Gaston Rivierre arrived there on his motorcycle, he had immediately been asked, "Jousselin, where is he?"

When he replied that, "He is in the front group with Garin and Aucouturier" a sort of delirium took hold of the crowd. Eyes misted over. A young lady pushed her way out of the group. It was Madame Jousselin, the happy wife of the young giant. When she learned that the riders were approaching, she ran and put a match under the vegetable soup prepared for her great man.

At 5:22 a.m., Jousselin and the others appeared. They were slightly behind schedule. Géo Lefèvre explained that the night had

114

been particularly black and had slowed their progress, this would have been less serious if they had not been hindered by an adverse wind as well.

The riders were back on the road to Rochefort and the next fixed control. Desgrange stayed glued to the leaders. He could see nothing irregular whatsoever. As the riders signed the sheet, there was no change in the leading group, apart from the disappearance of the Belgian Samson, whose real name was Lootens, hit by bad luck.

Desgrange relaxed a little. He was tempted to think that his presence was enough to prevent any incidents. But it came back to him that this had not put off the brigands at Saint-Etienne.

Desgrange, a former solicitor's clerk was already a respected leader in the world of sport and of motorcars. He had succeeded in turning his passion for cycling into a profession and even into a business. His talent and his exceptional stubbornness were recognized by all.

When he raced, it was under the strict code of an amateur that he embarked on his record attempts. Was it not he who made the first attempt at the unpaced world hour record? Even if it must be said that this record had been somewhat neglected at the time. He had covered 35.325 kilometers. The distance might seem to be modest, but not in the context in which it was achieved in 1893. When he was thirty, in 1895, he battled to win the 100 kilometer tricycle record, launching this outdated machine into one of its last combats.

His competitive pedaling career came to an end when this fanatical amateur agreed to preside over the professional riders union. It was true that the ease with which he coped with the complexities of law and his knowledge of the cycling scene automatically qualified him for the role. But there was a paradox. His nature as a patron tended to make him confront the riders rather than to defend them.

The tracks which as a rider he had abandoned, he rapidly returned to as a director. He found himself responsible for two velodromes, that of the East, for open air competition, and that of the winter, for inside pedaling. In his enthusiasm, he published a book which was immediately successful, *"La Tete et les Jambes"* ("The Head and the Legs"). It was an anthology of advice, written in the form of letters to a young cyclist.

At the same time, the specialized press picked up on it and he started to embroider it with discerning articles in the review *La Bicyclette*.

It is not possible to understand how Desgrange's career developed without understanding the position the bicycle held in the society of the time. The wealthy and even the aristocratic classes were attracted to the cycling phenomenon, seeing it as a natural progression to the horses which they had cherished so much. Posh people had eyes only for the bicycle. So in Paris, on the Avenue of the Grande Armee, thirty specialized shops opened their doors to the public. A group of sportsmen drawn from nobility came together to form the most select cycling club. This was to be L'Omium. It met in the most sumptuous hotel on the Rue Spontini, in the heart of the dashing 16th arrondissement. The Dukes of Luynes and of Brissac prided themselves on meeting there with the Viscount of Breteuil, the counts of Contades, of La Rochefoucauld and of Lorency, the duke of Uzes and the most powerful industrialists of the time. Did this brilliant association need a godfather? If so, it was supplied by the King of Portugal. Did it need a secretary to run things? This was to be... Henri Desgrange.

With his time taken up by his incessant duties, Desgrange was obliged to curtail his own personal cycling. It was only when he became well established in life that he started pedaling again. Then he began to run as well and even to swim long distances. He was to continue these athletic activities until an advanced age.

As we have seen, Henri Desgrange came up against Pierre Giffard, his main rival in the sporting press. But this conflict was never personal, as they both had high moral standards. Their rivalry was confined to commercial activities, exacerbated by Desgrange's backers, of whom the most important was the Count de Dion, the famous car maker. He even found himself opposed to Giffard in contesting a seat in the French parliament. This confrontation embraced the most animated terms, according to the political practices of the era, which lacked all elegance.

Desgrange also came up against a certain... Paul Bernard, the future Tristan of literature. The two "writers" crossed swords in their functions as... directors of velodromes. Paul Bernard could claim seniority in this field. He had been in charge of events at the Buffalo Velodrome at Neuilly from 1892, then at the arena of La

Seine de Levallois the following year. A new track had been constructed, the Velodrome of the East, in the woods of Vincennes. It can be imagined how little Paul Bernard appreciated the fact that the management of it was given to Henri Desgrange. He liked even less the tone that the latter adopted when in order to sing the praises of his reunions he said, "The new velodrome is rapidly becoming immensely successful. What a difference between its promotions and those of the Velodrome de la Seine or of the Buffalo, which are always dull and devoid of all interest."

Did he still have in his mouth the bitter taste of the misunderstanding of the Velodrome Mondesirat at Bordeaux? No sooner had it been announced that he was to be nominated as director, than he read in the newspaper that the post had gone to Desgrange.

This did not stop Paul Bernard from realizing the literary and theatrical career for which he is so well known. The two men did not hold these youthful rivalries against each other. In the 1930s, their two signatures were seen together, side by side, in the sumptuous album *"Joys of Sport."* Paul Bernard even followed the Tour de France for the daily press, leaving us his impressions in an agreeable book, *"Companion of the Tour de France."*

In 1904, in this, his 39th year, Henri Desgrange could consider that he had done quite well for himself. For the moment, he was traveling between Bordeaux and Nantes, looking very lively, in spite of a night without sleep. He had justified his unannounced presence as an immediate reaction against nails and broken bottles on the roads of the Tour de France. If ever he caught just one culprit....

After they had reached the half-way point of the stage, they headed for Rochefort, the next fixed control. The people of the A Ma Champagne Cafe appeared feverish. Just to think, the Tour de France in their home town! Suddenly they rose to their feet. Noise in the distance. It came closer. There they were! A big bold rider pushed himself forward. It was Jousselin. He obviously had acquired a taste for being the first to sign in. Ten other riders were still with him. They all decided to take time to feed themselves. The spectators noticed that for all that, they did not hang around.

At La Rochelle, after 244 kilometers, the crowd waiting for the heroes was enormous. When they arrived everyone was surprised to see their determined faces. Not one of them turned their heads to look at the sails of the fishing boats. Did they feel the sea air? As they were checked in, one rider was no longer with the leading group. It was Maitron.

It was now a long way to the signing in point at La-Roche-sur-Yon. It proved to be the end of the Tour for Gabory and Daumain. One man who did not want to suffer the same fate was hanging on to the skirts of the leaders. It was the only rider whose name had not yet appeared in the race communique, Charles Prèvost. So on each stage a new man was coming into the lime-light.

As the temperature was not too excessive, Maurice Garin and his band had kept on their white jackets. They were now leading the group. Aucouturier's red and blue striped jersey was often to be seen alongside Cornet's yellow jacket. These two riders, faced with the La Francaise trio were definitely seen as allies.

The finish was planned for the south of Nantes, in a busy sub-urb. Once again, Abran had taken his place and had things per-fectly in hand. As usual, a cafe was being used. It was situated 50 meters after the finishing line, and a quick glance was enough for the name to stick in the mind, Cafe du Velo. But the owner of the cafe did not think that that was enough and his establishment should really enter into the spirit of things. He had just repainted his sign, which now read "At the Finish of the Tour de France."

Which rider was he going to welcome first? Everyone agreed that it was going to be Aucouturier. The crowd was incredibly dense. The organizers had believed the crowd could be contained behind a rope. But most of them crossed over it. On the road the passage became very narrow and it was difficult for the riders to force their way through the crowds. Fortunately, a man arrived alone, fifteen lengths in front of his companions. "The Terrible." He was obviously strong. But what about the others? How would they share the other prizes? A rider with a red jersey came in, Dortignacq. A little further Charles Prèvost could be seen. The rider had held on! But what was this? He had fallen. The poor man had collided with Jousselin and Pothier. Silence reigned. He remained stretched out on the ground. They rushed towards him. He was bleeding from the head. Someone held a hand out to him. He could not take it. They carried him to a motorcar. It headed for the hospital. The diagnosis, a broken collar bone. The Tour de France was over for Prèvost. On the day of his glory!

He would not see the Cafe Continental where his comrades

had just signed in for a second time. This was the way it was. The double controls at the finish brought a few extra francs into the coffers of the race organization, all helping to pay the riders. Aucouturier was wildly acclaimed. Women threw flowers at him. One of the controllers quickly calculated the average speed for the 392 kilometers. He already knew that it would not be very high for the riders had been significantly behind schedule.

"23.250 kph," he announced.

No one took this as a sign of weakness. Everyone knew that a strong north wind had been blowing since Bordeaux.

One man did not worry about the average speed. He was happy not to have been involved in the crash involving Charles Prèvost. For him, it would have turned into a catastrophe. It was Garin. He remained first on the general classification. And the two following him belonged to his team, Pothier and his brother Cèsar. Delattre was delighted.

Sunday would be the final effort. As they waited, the gallant men had two days to sleep and recover their strength. But do not imagine that these men would remain locked up in their hotel. On the following day they were seen in the town followed by a crowd of children and pestered by the press. Le Petit Phare, Le Populaire and Le Nouvelliste were to be seen. When the top-class weekly, *La Vie Au Grand Air,* did not take the opportunity to supply its readers with informative prose, it exposed plate after plate to capture the riders on film strolling around the town.

Without question the most elegant was Garin, a man already well established in life. He was showing off an impeccable two piece suit, a superb tie was knotted over a white shirt with a wing collar. He could also claim the prize for the finest hat, wearing the very latest smart headware from England. Had it come from Jiel-Laval's shop at Bordeaux? All the riders were wearing caps, while in town straw hats were the most popular and the well-to-do had their bowler hats. These pedalers at rest were by no means all dressed the same. If Aucouturier had opted for a well-cut jacket with the plus-fours that were so dear to the hearts of cyclists, Cornet's garb was somewhat Chinese. He had slipped on trousers with turned-up bottoms and put on a jacket which had been ironed by his mother before the start of the race and by now had lost all its shape.

Aucouturier and Cornet were as close to each other in their

leisure as they had been on the road. They sat down on the terrace of a cafe, as they read L'Auto. They joked with a waiter wearing a long white apron. The three roadmen of La Francaise were equally inseparable. A happy Garin made an offer to his teammates: "Listen men, I'll pay for a ride in a carriage."

A coachman wearing a bowler hat showed off his town to them. Garin's good humor was understandable, he already smelled the big bundle of money that was going to be his. At the end of his cycling career he wanted to open a machinist's garage. He would not be the first to do this, all the former cycling champions were now in the automobile business.

The results of Stage 5 - Bordeaux - Nantes:

1.	Aucouturier	16 h 49 min 50 secs
	Bicycle - Peugeot	
	Tires - Michelin	
2.	Dortignacq	16 h 49 min 54 secs
3.	Garin, Cèsar	16 h 49 min 54 secs
4.	Cornet	16 h 50 min 1 secs
5.	Garin, Maurice	16 h 50 min 1 secs
6.	Pothier	16 h 50 min 8 secs
7.	Jousselin	16 h 50 min 14 secs
8.	Prèvost, Charles	16 h 50 min 20 secs
9.	Gabory	17 h 50 min
10.	Filly	18 h 37 min
11.	Daumain	18 h 37 min 5 secs
12.	Colsaet	19 h 53 min 15 secs
13.	Damalincourt	19 h 53 min 22 secs
14.	Dargassies	20 h 31 min
15.	Carrère	20 h 31 min

Stage distance - 392K (243 miles)
Winner's average speed - 23.25 kph (14.41 mph)

General Classification:

1.	Garin, Maurice	73 h 38 min 24 secs
2.	Pothier	73 h 38 min 52 secs
3.	Garin, Cèsar	75 h 26 min 37 secs

4. Cornet .... 76 h 26 min 50 secs
5. Aucouturier .... 76 h 30 min 45 secs
6. Dortignacq .... 78 h 53 min 59 secs
7. Jousselin .... 81 h 20 min 48 secs
8. Filly .... 85 h 24 min 6 secs
9. Gabory .... 87 h 28 min 42 secs
10. Dargassies .... 87 h 45 min 25 secs
11. Prèvost, Charles .... 91 h 17 min 39 secs
12. Maitron .... 91 h 51 min 10 secs
13. Carrère .... 93 h 41 min 10 secs
14. Samson .... 94 h 37 min
15. Chaput .... 97 h 17 min 4 secs

---

1 The "derby" was a common term for the Bordeaux-Paris race.
2 "Isoles" means "isolated ones".

Chapter 10
Nantes-Paris

"Monsieur Lefèvre?"

"Yes, that's me."

"A dispatch for you, Monsieur. It has come from Orleans."

"From Orleans? Give it to me."

Géo Lefèvre knew all about dispatches. He sent them, he received them. But why would someone send him one from a town situated on the route of the next stage of the Tour? He opened it. It read, "The scheming of the people from *L'Auto* will have its limits. The combines organized to help the rider of La Francaise win are going to stop. You made Beaugendre lose and retire at Bordeaux. You will pay for it at Orleans."

The remarks were, of course, anonymous. Géo Lefèvre remained frozen for a moment.

"It's not possible," he thought, "'they' are not going to start again!" he raged.

The "they" indicated all the brigands, the bandits, the hooligans, the embittered people, the enemies of the Tour de France. They were going to start demonstrating again! He looked into the distance, looking for an idea, something new, then a smile lit up his face. Was it something to do with the proverb "he who laughs last laughs loudest"?

From the day after the arrival at Nantes, everyone was fidgeting with impatience, the organizers as much as the riders. They were in a hurry to get to Paris, to release the pressure, to return to a more normal life. The stages had certainly done them some good. They slept well, the ate well. They had all tasted the local dishes. In the forefront were the riders of La Francaise. Delattre had taken them to the restaurants. They had been seen sitting down at the table in front of a turbot with white butter sauce, with a bottle of cold Muscadet close at hand. But for the moment this was behind them as they had to finish the race and get to Paris.

We would like to have made out the conversations between the men of La Francaise, but they did not filter through. Certain decisions had to be made. They had a choice. Let us not forget that Garin was only 28 seconds in front of Pothier! Just imagine a puncture close to the finish. Would Pothier wait for Garin or would he go on to pick up the winner's bouquet at the Parc des Princes? Curiously the journalists did not seem inclined to expand further on the subject. As for the public, their attention had been focused on Garin and Aucouturier and had been diverted by all the skulduggery.

It was on the last day that they began to sit up and take notice of the small margin between the first two riders. When it came to forecasting, Henri Desgrange always asked the same question, would Pothier regain the 28 seconds which separated him from Garin? The director of *L'Auto* remained totally impartial, probably in deference to the managers of La Francaise. On the other hand, he claimed that a struggle could now take place between the two riders.

While the prizes had been reduced and had not encouraged some of the best riders to start, the popularity of the Tour de France itself seemed to have grown by leaps and bounds. Géo Lefèvre wrote, "It is impossible to compare the success of the Tour de France at Nantes, this year, with that of last year. In 1903, the spectators came out of curiosity, but this time they are fired up with enthusiasm."

As usual the signing-in operation took place in a cafe, this time Le Continental, then they all moved on to another bar. Abran called the riders to the line. There were only thirty who replied to their names.

At seven o'clock in the evening, still daylight, they set off behind a Pothier who was feeling refreshed and challenged. It was noticed that the wind was favorable. The objective, Ville-d'Avray by the long way around, a total of 468 kilometers. The real finish would be the velodrome of the Parc des Princes, which would offer one last occasion for the riders to race against each other over two laps of the track, 666.6 meters.

The riders were being prudent. They were riding steadily. So at the first fixed control at Angers, after 89 kilometers, there was a leading group of 22. At Saumur, roughly 50 kilometers further on, there were still 17 of them. It goes without saying that all the leaders were in this group. The pleasant young Filly had signed in five minutes after the bunch but, as he lost no time at the control he was able to regain his place with the leaders. The man was beginning to catch scent of his own home town. He was from Loches. Soon they would be going through Tours where they were waiting for him.

The night was now at its darkest. In a village just after Saumur, a car was seen with its lights on. Its driver was taking some water from a fountain. Aucouturier saw what was happening. He shouted out to the others: "A fountain. Shall we stop for a moment?"

And the whole group braked as a single man. All except one -- Filly. He realized that this was his big chance to arrive at Tours by himself.

He was helped by the dark night. No one noticed his escapade. He was pedaling like a madman. The others, by reason of the fact that there were so many of them, took their time getting the water and then slowly restarted. So much so that the dropped riders were near. Twenty kilometers further on, when Filly turned around, he could not see even the slightest glimmer of a light in the distance. His pursuers were a long way behind. He shouted with joy. How surprised his mother would be. He increased the pace. At Langeais, in front of the chateau, someone recognized him and was flabbergasted. It was Filly alone in the lead!

He reached the outskirts of Tours. He kept turning around. No cyclists behind. When at 2:55 a.m., in the middle of the night, he pushed his way through the crowd, with a huge smile on his face, he was greeted by an enormous ovation. More than one thousand people had not hesitated to stay up to see the race go through. Here, they were used to waiting for riders in the middle of the night, since the Bordeaux-Paris had come into existence. Filly's incredulous parents were at the control. Their son was first! He embraced them and restarted among the cheers. The controller looked at his watch and stated that the minutes were ticking past. He counted 17 of them before a group of 14 riders arrived. It was a panic at the stations, they all wanted to sign in at the same time. The first to put his name down was astonished to see a name already on the sheet. The time gap surprised the other riders. But

124

after all there was still another 261 kilometers before they got to Paris. The signatures which followed that of Filly were those of: the Garin brothers, Pothier, Aucouturier, Jousselin, Catteau, Samson, Colsaet, Dortignacq, Rist, Drioul and Daumain, Colas and Cornet. Visibly, some of them were clinging to the leaders. But it was beginning to be noticed that as the stages went by, some riders were beginning to adapt and ride at the pace of the leaders.

At Amboise, Cornet was dropped by several minutes, following a mechanical incident. At the fixed control at Blois he had regained his place. And Filly as well, the group saw him again. But it was quite something for him not to be immediately dropped by the group after all his efforts. Everyone was glad to see the first signs of daybreak. As they signed in, the riders were told that the fixed control at Orleans had been cancelled and that they would be taking a different route through the town. This was Géo Lefèvre's answer to the dispatch he received at Nantes.

The situation at Orleans was such that no one had been informed of the change in plans. Not the controllers, nor the spectators, nor the journalists who had made the journey from Paris.

The staff from *La Vie Au Grand Air* were there in force. To them it was not unknown territory. Some of them knew the place very well indeed. For each Bordeaux-Paris, they arrived on the train, sat down in front of a glass of chocolate at the Hotel du Berry and awaited the race. This time, as the possibility of trouble could not be ruled out, they did not want to miss the spectacle. The cameras were ready. The journalist Victor Breyer was on the alert so as not to miss anything. Suddenly he was given a dispatch. It said that the riders were going to "burn"[1] the control. Victor Breyer was floored. The Orlean people were equally disappointed. They would not be seeing the riders. It was so much more a shame as everything seemed to be so calm here. Not the least sign of any demonstration. A spectator explained that the people of Orleans were peaceful and if a rider from the area had rightly or wrongly complained it was no reason for the organization to cancel everything. The head office of La Francaise had not been warned either. They had sent several dozen mechanics. Yes, several dozen. They all stood with their arms crossed.

During this time, the riders were racing along the road to Chartres. Not the smallest hill in sight. Then a shape appeared on the horizon, the famous cathedral. In this region where the week before the row of corn had stretched as far as the eye could see, only stubble was now on view. The harvest had been gathered.

The cathedral could be clearly made out, with its two spires, one finely carved, the other bare. A group of 13 riders entered the main city of the Beauce. The Cotterreau belonging to *L'Auto* preceded them. Abran was on board, with Lefèvre, Ouzou and his apprentice. They all looked a little curious with under their huge floppy hats which they had bought in the Midi region. They had folded the brims back as the sun was not overwhelming. The shopkeepers of Chartres, whose ancestors had financed the construction of the cathedral, had again been solicited for an appropriate gift - a prime for the riders. It was Aucouturier who picked up the prize. At the checkpoint, nothing had changed except that Filly was no longer with the leaders. He was nearly an hour down. He was paying for his efforts at Tours.

The monotonous route passed through Gallardon. However the road reared up before Rambouillet. Hills at last. But the group did not break up. There were still 13 riders. The situation was not to Aucouturier's liking. It was time to put things in hand. "The Terrible" drew up alongside Maurice Garin, and said, "There are too many of us. We've got to drop those who have been sitting on our wheels."

"I agree."

"Well, let's go then."

At once the blue and red striped jersey stretched out over the bike. The pace went up dramatically. The group stretched out. Three riders went off at Saint-Remy, then three others at Chateaufort. The Cotterreau, which had gone to the front, now arrived at the Arcades of Buc. About 15 men were in the middle of the road. The motor car was stopped. What were these men doing who were bending down? They were picking up the nails that some perverse hands had sown. Almost all of them were wearing plus-fours. They themselves were cyclists and, in their own way were demonstrating their solidarity with the champions.

When the riders went through, the road proved to be free of nails. Three men had gone clear, Aucouturier, Maurice Garin and Dortignacq. As for Pothier, he was down nearly three minutes. So the final issue of the Tour de France was being played out. Garin was finally fully establishing his superiority over Pothier. The hills in the Chevreuse valley were enough to do just that.

It would not be long before the outcome of the stage would be decided. It had been established that a first control would be organized at Ville-d'Avray and then the riders would contest two laps of the Parc des Princes. A superb supporting program had been put together, announced some time previously, and included gymnastics as well as cycling. The main race was to be a paced event with champions such as Michael, Guinard, Darragon and Valpic. But the sprint event was also an exceptional one, with the French Friol, Bourotte and Dupre and the Italians Gardellin and Bixio. If it was fine weather, the stands would be full to their bursting point, the organizer predicted, a certain... Henri Desgrange, the director of the velodrome.

The reasons for this double finish were mainly financial, although security reasons also played a part. An enormous crowd was expected at Ville d'Avray. No one had forgotten the finishes at Marseille and Nantes where the crowd had not been properly controlled and the sprint had been affected, even to the point where one rider had been sent to the hospital. The services of law and order had not provided enough men to control the situation. When the race had been on the road it had become mixed with horse-drawn vehicles, motorcars, and... bicycles. These two wheeled machines had been the worst, ridden by "pedards," incorrigible cyclists, with uncertain trajectories.

L'Auto had asked the riders to read carefully the following communique:

1) "At Ville d'Avray, there will be no delay but just a simple stop to receive the certificate showing the exact time that the neutralization will start for the rider;

2) One hour and 30 minutes exactly after the time recorded on the ticket, the entrance to the track, at which exact point the neutralized section will terminate, will be open to the competitor, being stipulated as in all automobile races, that he only commence his two laps one hour 35 minutes after or one hour 40 minutes after his arrival at Ville D'Avray, he will inevitably see his total time counting for the classification of the Tour de France augmented by five or ten minutes. Too bad for the rider who takes too long getting from Ville d'Avray to the Parc des Princes. The neutralization period is one hour 30 minutes and not one hour 35;

3) The total time counting for the general classification will be taken after two laps of the track, in other words only when the

race is finished;

4) Track bicycles will be authorized, for it is certain that all the Tour de France riders will find one of them at their disposal at the Parc des Princes;

5) Those who precede the riders will ensure that they travel from Ville d'Avray to the Parc des Princes on their bicycles, and not in a motorcar. If they do not conform to this rule they will be subjected to serious penalties."

Without doubt Garin and Aucouturier had read and reread these rules concerning the finish of this Tour de France. Their attitude, nourished by the desire to satisfy thousands of spectators on the hill of Picardie or those assembled around the race headquarters of "Father Auto," had without doubt saved the last finish from extreme confusion. They must not "crowd" the final struggle before performing at the velodrome. They were unable to stop themselves from climbing Picardie hill at top speed, digging deep into their reserves with their gears of six meters. Dortignacq could not follow them before they flew down the descent like madmen and emerged at the finish. Surprisingly, it was perfectly controlled by the gendarmes and the soldiers of the Versailles Engineers. Aucouturier had no trouble in outsprinting Garin by two lengths. Then Dortignacq arrived ten seconds down. They were followed by Pothier at three minutes, accompanied by Cèsar Garin, then their pursuers, such as Colsaet, Cornet and Samson.

This time, the rules remained the rules. The riders had to get to the nearby Parc des Princes by bicycle. Lefèvre and his team had already arrived there. After having crossed the track they parked their dusty Cotterreau on the grass. The public had given them a wild welcome, something quite unexpected. They were obliged to reply with a lap of honor. With the cheers ringing in his ears, Ouzou drove his motorcar the full 666.6 meters.

Fine weather had accompanied each of the stages of this Tour de France. Sometimes the sun had even burned the riders. Why could it not last a few more hours? But the sky was servant to no man and began to cloud over. Even worse a flash of lightning was seen. The velodrome was invaded by a smell of ozone and the rain began to fall. To negotiate the track would be difficult, as the turns were slippery. They decided to wait. Garin and the others were led to the sprinter's cabins. They waited stoically.

"We're going to get cold," was the only remark that they

could make.

The organizers were waiting for a break in the clouds before releasing the riders on the two laps of the track. But as it did not come, they decided to accept the finishing order at Ville d'Avray. A general consensus of opinion thought that this cautious choice was the right one.

The sky brightened up and Abran asked the roadmen if they wanted to go to the line to contest a "prime" for the two laps in question. Everyone agreed. The three specialists, Aucouturier, Cornet and Dortignacq went off quickly. At the bell Aucouturier made his move. Dortignacq was the first to be dropped, then Cornet lost contact as well. "The Terrible" carried it off. His victory was greeted by a huge ovation.

Maurice Garin, the winner of the Tour de France, was called on to ride a lap of honor. The band played a passionate "Marseillaise." His supporters could no longer be restrained and invaded the track center and carried him around in triumph. Seeing this, Aucouturier's fans seized their hero and raised him onto their shoulders. Then calm was restored. The trackmen could finish their event and the Tour de France riders could return to the riders' quarters. For them it was all over.

The consequences of this second Tour de France were already being assessed. Henri Desgrange was in the best position to perform the task. He was writing his piece for *L'Auto*. Humor was mixed with bitterness. His article began:

"THE END"

"The Tour de France has just finished and its second edition will, I fear, be the last. It will have died of its own success, of the blind passions which have been unleashed, of the abuse and of the suspicions that have come from ignorant and ill-intentioned people. And yet, however, it seemed to us and it still seems that we had built, with this great event, the most durable and the most imposing monument to cycle sport. We had hoped to each year bring a little more sport across the greater part of France. The results of last year showed us that our reasoning was correct and here we are at the end of the second 'Tour de France', sickened and discouraged, having lived through these three weeks of the worst slander and abuse.

"And of all those who have grovelled to us, they have perhaps not been too sensitive to our feelings and have demonstrated their childishness and stupidity and have yet wished to make us their associates, what am I saying? The representatives of one of the companies who took part in the race. Simple good sense and plain dignity meant that we had to maintain our independence in a race where we had invited all the constructors, not to favor one to the detriment of the others. But no! Nothing worked out, all our acts were misrepresented. The same punishment inflicted on a rider was treated like a pitiless act and as a significant weakness. Let us be quite clear, we were considered to be barbarians, we willingly kept our eyes closed in order to see nothing....

"So we will provisionally leave to others, the care of confronting the adventures similar to a 'Tour de France' and for next year we will study what can be done in the way of other ideas. Also between now and then public opinion will perhaps change: perhaps the thing that inspired everybody to cheat during these last races on the road will be a salutary lesson in itself; perhaps people will acquire the habit of recognizing cheating where it really exists and not everywhere and especially where it is not. Finally, before coming to the results of the race, I will finish by affirming that if we did not suppress all the fraudulent acts which took place in the 'Tour de France', we did punish all those for which we had clear proof; and by clear proof, I do not mean the wild accusations of a contestant, or an ignorant person or someone with an axe to grind. I will add that there is still time for us to punish all those proved to be guilty, for the complaints register will remain open for another three days."

This register was to be delivered to three men, the race commissaries. To them fell the formidable honor of establishing a dossier in order to ratify the race. For the moment, here are the results of the final stage, Nantes-Paris.

1. Aucouturier .... 19 h 28 min
   Bicycle: Peugeot
   Tires: Michelin
2. Garin, Maurice .... 19 h 28 min
3. Dortignacq .... 19 h 28 min 10 secs
4. Pothier .... 19 h 31 min
5. Garin, Cèsar .... 19 h 31 min
6. Colsaet .... 19 h 32 min
7. Cornet .... 19 h 33 min

8. Samson	19 h 47 min	
9. Colas	19 h 48 min	
10. Jousselin	20 h 11 min	
11. Drioul	20 h 25 min	
12. Rist	20 h 30 min	
13. Daumain	20 h 54 min	
14. Catteau	21 h 48 min	
15. Dargassies	21 h 53 min	
16. Carrère	21 h 55 min	
17. Maitron	23 h 21 min	
18. Gautier	23 h 21 min	
19. Filly	23 h 21 min	

Final classification:

1. Garin, Maurice	93 h	6 min	24 secs
2. Pothier	93 h	9 min	52 secs
3. Garin, Cèsar	94 h	57 min	27 secs
4. Aucouturier	95 h	58 min	50 secs
5. Cornet	96 h	5 min	55 secs
6. Dortignacq	98 h	22 min	
7. Jousselin	101 h	40 min	6 secs
8. Catteau	105 h	7 min	20 secs
9. Filly	108 h	43 min	6 secs
10. Dargassies	109 h	10 min	25 secs
11. Samson	114 h	24 min	
12. Maitron	115 h	12 min	10 secs
13. Carrère	115 h	30 min	40 secs
14. Daumain	118 h	50 min	31 secs
15. Colsaet	119 h	50 min	13 secs
16. Colas	121 h	15 min	45 secs
17. Saget	122 h	1 min	11 secs
18. Drioul	127 h		44 secs
19. Paret	128 h	24 min	34 secs
20. Gautier	129 h	19 min	57 secs
....			
27. Deflotriere	197 h	34 min	47 secs

---

1 Pass by a fixed control without stopping to sign in but done with the permission of the organizers.

Chapter 11
Garin Feted

They were called Hesse, Gatoux and Levasseur. They were the race commissaries. One of them liked cycle sport, while another was a privileged person of his federation and a third saw the position as an opportunity to attend a few banquets. Is this not the normal type of representation on sporting bodies? It is impossible to attribute to them any tendency of affection. No one can remember now which of them liked the sport, his federation or his stomach. Yet their mission consisted of investigating the complaints and taking note of the irregularities. Would they stumble on a riddle as they proceeded with their inquiries? As there were no scientific tools available, they would have to rely solely on witnesses. Their role consisted of flushing out after the fact, the cheat, as far as they could. They were not, in fact, judges. They would submit their dossier to the U.V.F. who would in their turn give a verdict. Another sporting affair was waiting for a ruling, that of the Bordeaux-Paris, organized by *Le Velo* and it was known that it had been subjected to nails in the road and other villainy.

Here the ground was safer. When the boil had to be lanced, Desgrange and Lefèvre had not hesitated. Some riders had been penalized and others excluded from the race. But as their main concern was to preserve the event itself had they always been totally objective?

There was something new. The journalist Desgrange, who showed himself to be rather prophetic on the comportment of certain riders, appeared to be more loquacious in his appraisal. After having congratulated the La Francaise team for its three leading riders, he could not prevent himself from adding certain qualifications.

"While congratulating them on a success which their three

champions were perfectly capable of achieving by their worth, I would like to address a reproach in all friendliness: it is that of having confided the organization of the "Tour de France" to some-one too previously involved in the unfortunate events which always accompany races on the road, having neither the calmness nor the independence of character, nor the foresight needed to understand that a new situation was born from the dislike of frauds committed in races on the road.

"This representative, I will not identify him exactly, for all those who are involved with races on the road know him perfect-ly, has been, and I am not afraid to say it, a very clumsy flag-bear-er. Persuaded that the cheating was going to begin again, he took precautions not only to defend the team against them but yet, and I could not swear to it, to reply to them as well. All along the route he has been bending the rules, giving the impression that he believed in the axiom that it is never forbidden to do wrong, but only never to be caught. Let us not exaggerate, he has nothing against his name, I have received no complaint about him and I do not believe he has done anything wrong. But he has brought down on the heads of the riders, who it was his duty to defend in the con-trols, all the anger and all the hate of their adversaries as well as that of the public. It was he who they saw everywhere and, by a very human injustice, even where he could not possibly be."

The anonymous representative was easy to recognize. It was Delattr, the team manager. So here was Desgrange making a rod for his own back. Admittedly a Desgrange devastated by the dis-appointment caused by the iconoclasts of his own great achieve-ment. But had Desgrange taken into account that his observations could only have a negative effect on the dossier that was to be built up for the U.V.F.?

Henri who cried on Monday would laugh on Tuesday. Morale returns quickly to a man of his caliber. He had scarcely put this Tour de France to bed than he started thinking about making another attempt. After just one day's reflection.

He had realized that his task was not finished and that the organization of the event needed to be improved. "It would be ridiculous, when launching such a considerable undertaking, one with such detailed complications, to pretend to have achieved per-fection at the first attempt," he said.

After having listed the Tour's weaknesses, he provided the

remedies. "In brief, finishes far from the towns, a complete time-keeping service, more scruples from the driver who accompanies or the inquisitive cyclists following the race, and the deletion of nighttime stages, constitute the improvements that we would try to implement in a third edition of the Tour de France."

It is interesting to note that Desgrange used the conditional tense in an ostentatious way; the reader of *L'Auto* would think it unseemly that he could so easily and so quickly perform a total about-face. By the virtue of his grammar, Desgrange was attempting to tone down his change of mood. He did not want to demonstrate the length of time he had spent reflecting on the subject, perhaps even before the finish at the Parc des Princes.

For the riders it was "settling up" time. The La Francaise and the Peugeot company had announced some generous bonuses as their riders had ridden very well. Let us not talk about Garin and Pothier whose first and second places speak for themselves. But Aucouturier, if he was unfortunate on the first day, had all the same won four stages out of six! J.C., the little Parisian bicycle manufacturer who equipped the young Cornet, was equally satisfied. Their rider was using a "sealed" machine and he changed nothing during the course of the race. It was a proof of quality that deserved to be publicized. They were also given a quarter of a page ad in *Le Velo* which claimed that beyond all doubt, Cornet was the moral winner of the Tour de France.

On top of the renu,erations of the bicycle companies, there were the prizes to be added. Maurice Garin won 6,000F, Aucouturier 2,500F, Cèsar Garin 2,000F and Cornet 700F. All that remained was for the U.V.F. to give their approval before they were paid.

All of these men were in a state of euphoria. Their attendence was wanted everywhere. They began on Monday by visiting the offices of *L'Auto*. The elder Garin was surprised to find a message waiting there for him from a sculptor, Maximin Joany, who offered to make a bust of him. He came across Beaugendre, the rider from Salbris, who had retired at Bordeaux in order to protest what he saw as irregularities against him on the part of the two brothers.

"Everything all right, Beaugendre?"

"Yes, yes, the business at Bordeaux was nothing. My manager regretted his complaint. And I... my retirement. I could never imagine that friends of mine could so disrupt the checkpoint at

Orleans. It's a shame that because of this the riders were diverted from the control. They would have been well received. Anyway, Maurice, I congratulate you, you deserved your victory."

No one contested Maurice Garin's win. They all now wanted to celebrate it with him. He would have to rearrange his calendar in order to accept as many invitations as he could. Along with Pothier, he began by accompanying his brother Cèsar to his home in Wattrelos in the north. As they got off the train at Roubaix station, the three men were met by the local people and led through a swirling, noisy crowd, with music provided by several local bands. Then they went to Sens where Pothier was welcomed by his compatriots. Just think, a second place behind the famous Garin! The master cyclist had to wait until the end of the week to benefit from a sumptuous reception laid on by his municipality. During all these festivities, Delattre never left either him or his entourage, always putting La Francaise first. At Lens, he murmured into Garin's ear. "We too, are going to celebrate this fine victory and... at Paris. The owner has just reserved a big restaurant. There will be 30 of us. So with the invited journalists, the public will really know the name of La Francaise!"

During this time a large amount of mail arrived at Rue Montmartre. Ordinary people as well as notable ones had been supporting Desgrange and imploring him to reconsider his decision of no longer organizing the Tour de France. Several critical letters arrived as well. Mr. Hammond, the director of La Francaise, who Desgrange had reproached for not having ordered Pothier to attack Garin, defended himself in these terms, "I have just read your criticism of Pothier for not having tried to drop Maurice Garin.

"You are speaking about it at your ease, but why did you not address the same reproach to Aucouturier, who according to you was superior? An Aucouturier who in almost all the stages was content to gently follow the leading group, saving himself to beat the others on the line, so that we saw three stages of 500 kilometers reduced to matches of just a few hundred meters!

"The truth, that you yourself should publish, is that none of the riders dared trying to free themselves for fear of playing into the hands of the others and sacrificing his own chances by making the terrible effort that was required.

"Pothier, Aucouturier and the others remembered that

Maurice Garin cannot be left behind with impunity and the story of Lesna in Paris-Brest was not lost on them. So you speak loosely when you talk of Maurice Garin's easy victory. Perhaps they could have beaten him, but none of them did, that is all there is to it."

It was true that the eldest of the Garins demonstrated a reserve strength and they were always afraid that he might "get the whip out."

Without yet knowing what the Tour de France was going to generate by way of advertising spin-offs, increased sales of *L'Auto*, and "contributions" from the establishments chosen for the control sites, the newspaper begam trying to work out the cost of the event. The money given in prizes to the riders was already known, more than 22,000F. To this had to be added the expenses of the controls, Abran's expenses, putting up the course signs and the direction arrows, the dispatches from one control to another, keeping watch on the route, etc. The total budget was estimated to be 40,000F. Measured by the fact that each edition of *L'Auto* was sold at 5 centimes and in a context of a limited money supply, it was a fair budget, but no more than that.

They counted on a lot in 1904. That which was owing, remained so. And nothing remained in the shadows. Some spectators had lent equipment to the poor cyclists who were forbidden by the rules from receiving help from their teams outside the controls. It now remained to return these bikes and these wheels. The address to which the machine had to be returned, that had been borrowed by the Belgian Lombard at Saint-Etienne, was indicated to him. Catteau was asked if he could remember where the bicycle was that had been handed over to him at Rambouillet. The reverse happened as well. Aucouturier had put on a front wheel at the disposition of a helpful person who had lent him one during the first stage.

The Friday after the Tour, on the stroke of five in the evening, Messrs. Hesse, Gatoux and Levasseur passed through the archway leading to the offices of *L'Auto*. They had come to investigate the file of complaints. They were not to go back through the arch in the opposite direction until well into the night, somewhat confused. They had adjourned, postponing their decision until the following Monday. But already they had made it known that the ratification of the results would in all likelihood be delayed, for several complaints made a detailed enquiry necessary.

The following Monday they only concluded that they needed more time to complete their dossier. Then a long silence fell on the proceedings. No one talked any longer about the Tour de France. None of the public imagined what had happened in the legal domain and that the results would be decided around the table.

The beginning of August, Garin and his teammates were feted at the Dehouve Restaurant, by their boss and the head office of the firm La Francaise. Desgrange, Lefèvre, and most of the Parisian sports editors were present at the banquet. When the dinner was over, Garin was permanently given the a commemorative cup from *La Vie Au Grand Air* for his second victory in the Tour de France. Garin particularly appreciated the fact that he had won two Tours de France.

The time went by. *L'Auto* justified its title more and more by supplying hundreds of details on the Motor Show which was being prepared and which would reveal itself in all its pomp and splendor in the Great Palace, just off the Champs Elysees. During this time, *Le Velo* was dying on its feet. It folded on the 20th of November, 1904.

Just before, its directors had been approached by a consortium who wanted to move into the newspaper business. Their idea was to concentrate on the motor car in the same way as *L'Auto* was doing. The very idea made *Le Velo* shudder, seeing themselves condemned in this way. Fortunately, the consortium, calling itself the "New Society of Sporting Journals," although with considerable capital at its disposal, became frightened at the idea of starting from scratch and thought it would be wiser to benefit from the established structure of *Le Velo*. In brief, it absorbed it, keeping its offices, its editor and its best journalists, among whom was Tristan Bernard. The green paper it was printed on became pink, and *Le Velo* became *Journal de L'Automobile*, while under the main title appeared the words "Of Cycling and of All Sports." They too started to get ready for the Motor Show.

This Motor Show turned to the advantage of Desgrange, although he was in no way a "driver." Although no one mocked him for this; he had just learned that his position was recognized by the fact that he was to be given the Cross of the Knight of the Legion of Honor. He would receive his honor along with Armand Peugeot and Adolphe Clement, two well known industrialists in the motor construction business. Also he was not too worried about the U.V.F. not yet having ratified the result of the Tour de France. For him, the U.V.F. was an organization with limited authority. The real power was in other hands, such as the industrialists and the bankers. Incidentally, it was these types of people he mixed with more and more, inciting them to undertake more. So his attention was focused on the 7th of December, the opening day of the Motor Show. That is not to say that he neglected the pedaling machine. This was also a bicycle show and - as much as they needed one - not every Frenchman yet had his own bike. A large popular market existed which was close to a million bicycles a year. The activities of the bicycle and the motor car became closely interwoven, and most motor manufacturers had a bicycle department. There was not one champion or cycle constructor from the previous decade who had not turned to the motor car in one form or another.

So the U.V.F. was present at the Motor and Cycle Show. It decided that it was imperative to produce the results of its enquiry into the Tour de France before the show opened so that the manufacturers could gain the maximum publicity from the results. More than 300,000 people were expected to attend!

Chapter 12
Garin Disqualified

Wednesday, November 30. At the headquarters of the Union Velocipedique de France. They had decided to put a stop to it all. To all the cyclists who had cheated in road races. They had had enough of riders who did not respect the rules, who climbed in motorcars and then got out again just before the control and then threw nails in the road behind them. They had had enough of their managers who encouraged them to cheat so that the manufacturers' names could be seen at the top of the classification table.

Already the Sporting Commission had acted ruthlessly in the case of Bordeaux-Paris. The first four riders were simply disqualified. It had not been totally established if they were the only culprits in the race, but they were excluded from the results... and the prizes. Exit Leon Georget, the first man home in 18h 47 minutes and Muller, far behind in 21 hours and 11 minutes. Augereau had been preferred to them, who had been 4 hours 30 minutes down on the first man. At the U.V.F. there was no room for the least doubt. Even if those disqualified appeared to be more likely the victims of independent combinations than guilty themselves!

But there was another file for the Tour de France. And it was not a thin one. It contained the report of the three commissaries and two filing cabinets full of complaints, listed under nine separate headings. The U.V.F. came to the conclusion that the contents excluded an official communique. It decided not to do its dirty laundry in public. Was this to protect cycle sport from an even bigger scandal? Just imagine revealing that one rider had ridden in a car, and that another had ridden 50 kilometers behind the shelter of another car. The public would not be able to take it in. The thought of bringing everything to light frightened them. They would not do it. Sentences would be handed down but the reasons would not be given. Unfortunately, later, it would be impossible to check that these sentences were justified, as the dossier disappeared.

An appendage to this story allows us to go into the complete communique of the U.V.F. The most important points of the decision were explosive. The first four finishers were disqualified and Cornet was declared the winner. These four riders were to lose the benefit of all their results. But this was nothing, the sanctions were taken even further. Pothier was disqualified for life and Garin excluded from all racing for a period of two years. As a consequence, the classification of the six stages was reviewed and corrected. Exit the Garins, Aucouturier and Pothier, winners on the road. And welcome (?) Frederick, Faure, Cornet, Beaugendre and Dortignacq, all with stage wins handed to them on a silver plate.

Cornet, declared the overall winner, received the main prize of 5,000F, plus some minor prizes that went with it. He did not complain. "Cornet the Joker" found the situation amusing. As for Garin, he received nothing at all and, even worse, his honor was stained. "The Little Chimney Sweep" was a fake! The decision of the U.V.F. turned out to be most serious as much for him as for... the organizer of the event, who was also censured. The two men reacted immediately. But in different ways. Maurice Garin, deprived of a platform would find it difficult to defend himself; the extent of his rage did not reach the country areas. For Henri Desgrange, on the other hand, his outrage was formulated. In *L'Auto*. Using his legal background, he wrote, "It is extremely difficult to establish whether the heavy punishments handed out by the U.V.F. to the principle riders were motivated by serious reasons, when we are given only the results of these decisions while at the same time the documents which they used are withheld from us.

"It is no exaggeration to say that public opinion will demand from the Union Velocipedique some explanation, which will no doubt be forthcoming. As for us, we have had recourse to it as to a supreme power, an entirely independent power, well qualified, the only one, in the last resort, qualified to settle such a delicate affair regarding a sporting event, which during the period of a month, caused the public to be overcome with emotion.

"We are convinced, until we are proved to be wrong, and I am sure that this will never be the case, we are convinced that the sporting commission has judged with its soul and with its conscience and that this conscience is entirely clear. I believe however, and I will tell you why, I believe that it has made a big mistake by sanctioning in this way, a race of the magnitude of the Tour de France.

"It is said that they have gone against the spirit and the letter of the rules.

"In front of me, the heads of the two big companies which were affected by the verdict of the U.V.F., gave all their personal attention to the race, they gave strict instructions that all rules should be observed at all times. I personally followed two stages and can confirm that no fault, no fraud was committed by any of the riders of these two makes which merited such repression.

"I would add that the dossier that the race commissaries transmitted to the U.V.F., contained no facts which deserved to be punished so heavily and that, if the inquiry conducted by the U.V.F. has uncovered some unknown facts, it owes it to the public and to the manufacturers concerned, to publish them.

"And as is now right and proper to say, now that the sentences have been pronounced, I would personally have judged otherwise, while agreeing with the disqualification of Chevalier and Payan, who were both caught redhanded, I would have caused Pothier to suffer the same fate.

"To the others, I would have distributed a number of fines; I really believe that they did not deserve more.

"It remains for the U.V.F. to prove the opposite to the public, to those who I call the victims, and to the manufacturers and to prove that they know how to make a distinction between the spirit and the letter of the rules."

We are a long way from Emile Zola's famous letter, "J'Accuse!" Desgrange did not dare to strike back too hard. It was as if he had several small wrongs to reproach himself with. Wrongs which remain unknown to us, with the exception of the Pothier affair. He was being ambiguous, he inferred at the beginning of his article that he did not perhaps know of all the misdemeanors and then later claimed that he knew the contents of the file of complaints.

The U.V.F. maintained its stony silence. There was no appeal against its judgement. The *Journal de L'Automobile*, successor to

Le Velo, although a fierce rival of *L'Auto* and a declared enemy of Desgrange, was itself annoyed and did not hesitate to fly to the aid of the organizer of the Tour de France. Its director and chief editor, Gaston de Pawlowski, no doubt given a free hand, began by making a direct attack on the shallow minds of those in the U.V.F. who had not taken into account the consequences of their acts.

He wrote, "Order reigns in the U.V.F. - After the Bordeaux-Paris executions, those of the Tour de France were expected and one can say that nobody was surprised.

"Today order reigns in the world of sport just as it has reigned for a long time in the Pere-Lachaise cemetery.

"Moreover, I am certain that the U.V.F. judged with great impartiality and believed that justice had been done when it reached its verdicts, severe though they were.

"Unfortunately, it must be said, absolute justice is not of this world, and if we believe in an old precept, maximum justice is sometimes and at the same time, the height of injustice."

Gaston de Pawlowski went on to add that "the disqualification of the first four was no guarantee of the honesty of those who followed them home, especially if they had not been closely watched. If they appeared to be as white as snow, it was simply because people had paid less attention to them. And why should they, if they were not at the forefront of the race!" He continued. "I know full well that in matters of sport only facts are important and can be taken into consideration. It is however no less true that in all fairness, we know that certain riders are better than others and that there will always be 'moral winners' of an event, no matter what the final classification....

"It is often not a question of being right, but there is also the 'manner', and it is this manner which it seems to us to be more and more escaping those who direct cycle sport in France. It is a situation which cannot but avoid attracting the attention of the employer's federations of the motor and the cycle trade, because it could, in the long run, become particularly harmful and dangerous....

"The U.V.F. is not, as it believes, a 'simple tribunal' charged with judging and condemning. Above and beyond that, it must first of all be a 'society of encouragement' creating and organizing cycle sport in France.

"The day when it cancels and says that all cycle races held in our country are impossible, it may well be a fair judgement, but it is at the same time judging itself and signing its own death warrant.

"We do not need friends who will criticize us, even if they are right, without at the same time coming to our aid.

"We have enough enemies."

His reply must have pleased Desgrange. What he did not appreciate was the silence of the U.V.F.

As the file of complaints - opened at his request - remained at *L'Auto* for several days, he had all the time in the world to study it and gain some idea of the extent of the cheating. It also notably cast light on the manner in which the stages had been run which he had not followed. So in a second article, he declared himself to be still very astonished at the severity of the sanctions.

"I indicated on Friday morning how rigorous these penalties seemed, even to me who knew what was in the complaints file, when it was transmitted to the Sporting Commission and I asked the U.V.F. to take the heat out of the situation by publishing the reasons for the disqualifications which they had just published.

"But with total indifference and I would even say lack of concern, the U.V.F. did not move, thus running away before an inevitably large storm. They were very wrong in not thinking that very serious and diverse interests are involved in events like Bordeaux-Paris and the Tour de France.

"They know full well that there is no question of publishing the entire voluminous file of complaints on the Tour de France, but they should make known to the interested parties the reasons for these decisions. And by interested parties, I do not mean only the riders, but the intermediaries, the constructors and even *L'Auto* itself, which at the appropriate time received all the complaints but could not see how they could lead to such executions. All it would need to settle the affair would be a meeting lasting just a couple of hours between a few people. If a member of the Sporting Commission would say that the decisions taken were reached by a unanimous verdict of the fifteen present, it would not be difficult to convince all those people who doubt that the U.V.F. is a just and impartial body.

"We are no longer in the time of the "Credo quia absurdum"[1], and their judicial powers, such as they are, only have as much authority as motivates their judgements.

"And the U.V.F. is still in a position to do it without appearing to give way to any pressure.

"It does not alter the fact that Maurice Garin was set upon and beaten on the Col du Grand Bois! And yet his well-deserved 6,000F was taken from him. Even worse, the two year-suspension imposed on him will put an end to his career, as he is now 34 years old. He should never accept his disqualification."

Fifty years later...

What was happening here? Everyone was excited. What a lot of people in front of the hotel! A poor mounted policeman could not cope. Young soldiers in dark red trousers are amused. It is not their place to restore order. A woman whose skirt brushes the ground is laughing under her parasol. A photographer with a straw hat on his head and his legs hidden by plus-fours was using his black box to his heart's content. Such was the spectacle on this day at the end of June in front of the "Au Hotel Reveil Matin!"

A shiver ran through the crowd.

"They're coming!"

It was the riders. They came into sight. On their right arms, a yellow armband with embroidered gothic letters: L'Auto. Well, well, here was the rider number 24, towards whom three journalists dashed, ties around their necks and straw hats protecting their heads. Their questions came one after the other. The rider they were interrogating, a fine looking man with rather full cheeks was breathing no harder than if he had just come back from a training ride. His bike, with wide La Francaise handlebars, was nevertheless the very latest thing. Another candidate for sporting glory, with a red and white striped jersey, was rummaging through his handlebar bag and joking with a young teenage girl. He had taken the goggles off his eyes and moved them up to his jockey's cap. Folding chairs had been arranged in front of the hotel, occupied by smartly dressed gentlemen. The officials, no doubt.

But who was this singing, down there? A street singer had distributed some small sheets of music. A very "chic" lady, under a hat loaded down with peaches, broke into song. Her neighbor, with a bowler hat, was singing another song, "Long live the Tour de France"! Many youths, strapping fellows with magnificent moustaches and ladies swishing elegantly around. If these riders had not been dripping with sweat under their dusty jerseys, this

144

could have been the start of the race.

Three old gentlemen looked a little out of place here, they were too old for bicycles! And then, they were strangely attired. They did not look as if they were interested in the fashions of the day. But look, two of them were displaying the rosette of the Legion of Honor! The one who seemed to be the eldest had the weather-beaten face of a worker, or perhaps a retired peasant. How could he have won this distinction?

There was a ripple of applause. It was for him. They had recognized him, it was Maurice Garin, 82, and Lucien Pothier, 69, a mere youth, and Géo Lefèvre, 76. "The Little Chimney Sweep" had not gotten any bigger, but he had kept the magnificent moustache of the days of his glory. The large cap that he is wearing with his fine light suit and dark tie looks like his Sunday best without being too elegant. When the photographer gets hold of him, he sunk down a little and his arms froze to his sides. Géo Lefèvre took his position between him and Lucien Pothier. His two hands placed on the shoulders of the two historic companions, brought them together just as if one of them did not exist without the other, but also it was as if neither of them could have belonged to prosperity without him.

In this way, Pothier was invited to the celebrations. The disgrace of 1904 was blurred. And, if he was carrying a small suitcase, let us not believe that he had just come out of prison! His three-piece suit, his white pocket handkerchief, his gold watch chain, all were proof of a certain social success.

In order for the commemoration to be complete, they had brought an old car which had been discovered and which was built at the beginning of the century and Maurice Garin got in. When the driver started off, he lifted his cap and waved to the crowd. The old Maurice was visibly gratified. He remembered his first two Tours de France when he started on the road to Lyon, as if it were yesterday. He was happy to see the "Butcher of Sens" again and the kind organizer of 1904 who fed them with chicken.

Géo Lefèvre said to him, "Maurice, this is not everything, the celebrations for the 50th anniversary of the Tour do not stop here. They will continue up until the end of the Tour. Do you want to come to the finish? You can congratulate the winner there and the public will be delighted."

"That's fine by me, Géo, but do not ask too much of me. I'm

no longer very strong, age has had its effect."

"I know something about that! So, I'll see you at the Parc des Princes?"

"At the Parc des Princes."

All of France joined in the rhythm of the Tour de France. One of its own citizens was in the process of winning it. A popular man who had until this time come up against the other champions of his era, such as Coppi, Bartali, Koblet and Kubler. This time, Louison Bobet had completed the worst of this year's Tour. He just had to keep his jersey until the Parc des Princes was reached.

He was greeted with wild acclaim. The elegant rider from Brittany was radiant in his yellow jersey embroidered with the initials H.D., in memory of Henri Desgrange. He had been told that Maurice Garin was going to come to salute him. It was the moment that he was waiting for. The old man came to him, led by Géo Lefèvre. The first winner of the Tour de France had kept the suit and cap by which he was known but had changed into a fine paisley tie of light silk.

This meeting was not lacking the expected emotion. It was mainly looks that passed between them. Garin slowly held out his right hand, seized that of Bobet and held on to it. He congratulated his young successor in the most solemn way that he could. His eyes shone, fed by a vitality that most people believed he no longer possessed. The height of the rider from Brittany meant that he had to put his head back to look him in the face. He looked hard at him, however, as if trying to make him out. Then for a moment he settled down and asked himself the essential question. Was there a structural difference between them? The new man who certainly went faster than he, was he better than the old one? And if so, why? Where did this extra athletic ability come from? Garin went no further in his reflections. He became sentimental. A paternal glow lit up his face.

Bobet was no less attracted to the old champion but he was engulfed with the happiness of the day and could go no further with the dialogue. For the moment an essential fact drew the two men together - respect. That which only heroes could share.

A photographer took advantage of the occasion. Géo Lefèvre said to Garin, "We'll send you the photo, Maurice."

"I'm counting on it, Géo."

The photo finally reached Lens. Maurice Garin looked at it

for a long time. Ah, this handshake with Bobet! Then he took his pen and wrote on the back "Fiftieth anniversary of the Tour de France 1903 = 1904-1953." And he signed it: "Maurice Garin." It was a remarkable business. The former ace had just drawn the equal sign after the date of the first Tour de France and had then added 1904. The photo was religiously preserved.

So in this way he proved that he had never accepted the fact that his name had been removed from the results of the 1904 Tour.

The Tour de France that he had won. He should never have been deprived of it.

---

1 "Credo quia absurdum," means "truth over stupidity."

147

Chapter 13
Beyond 1904

These days it would be right and just to re-establish Maurice Garin as victor and to reclassify his brother Cèsar and Aucouturier, behind him and immediately in front of Cornet. As Desgrange said, only Pothier should be disqualified. He should never have been allowed to start the second stage, his serious faults on the first day should have excluded him. But the ban on him racing for the rest of his life should have been lifted as it violated his right to work. Perhaps Pothier should have been told that he should consider himself lucky - at least they had not condemned him to death!

The tumults of July continued right up until December. After that Desgrange regained his equilibrium, he once again threw himself into his main passion. From the spring, he sent Abran off to report on the viability of a new Tour with eleven stages in place of six. All run during the day. In fact, during the middle of the day. Since then the Tour de France has only been interrupted by war.

What about Garin? As he had always planned, he opened a mechanic's garage in Lens. When the establishment was baptised, he was not embarrassed to call it "The Champion of the Road." He certainly was not exaggerating.

During this period of change, he still enjoyed cycling, especially over long distances. Certainly he had moved on to other things. But when, in 1911, the Paris-Brest-Paris was reborn after the usual gap of 10 years, he put his name down for it, as he was the previous winner. In spite of his 40 years of age, he still felt capable of getting to the finish in a good position. He put on his old racing clothes, complete with white jacket --- and finished tenth. Now he could really enjoy his retirement from the sport! From here and there he continually received signs of esteem. The 50th anniversary of the Tour de France, in 1953, was one of them, even though he still had painful memories of 1904. He was 82. Behind his rather touching Sunday best, the old man still had a lively expression. He left this world one day in February, 1957, in his 86th year.

And what about the others, the essential personalities of this 1904 adventure, the riders Aucouturier, Cornet, the little Filly, the journalists and the organizers, Desgrange, Abran, what became of them? How did they end up?

Aucourturier had not been disqualified by the U.V.F. He was seen again on the roads in 1905, always battling. He won the Bordeaux-Paris, his race. Then came the Tour de France, run to a new formula, with no pedaling during the night. He struggled fiercely against Trousselier, Georget and Petit-Breton, all riders of the next generation. Once again had to give his best, this time behind Trousselier. His chance had disappeared. There were just places of honor for him. He died in 1944.

"Cornet the Joker" was not the weakling that he was made out to be after he finished several hours behind Garin in 1904. Could you imagine that he won the Paris-Roubaix in 1906 and wa again on the podium in this very same race as well as others such as Bordeaux-Paris and Paris-Tours.

And in the Tour de France? He was to shine less here, because the standard of racing had gone up considerably. But all the same, he managed some very honorable places: 8th, 11th, 16th. Hardened by the years but keeping his speed, he rode the 24-hour Bol d'Or. He took some very fine places. Would he attempt the long and languid Paris-Brest-Paris in 1911? Most certainly. And he only just missed being on the podium. His life came to an end in 1941, in a little village in Eure-et-Loire.

Filly, the surprising Camille Filly, the 17-year-old kid who took on the greats and put up with the sleepless nights in 1904. He should have been the man to watch in the following years. He started "The Big Loop" in 1905 but was hardly brilliant, but did honor to his youth by finishing in the 14th rank. But he was nev-era able to take his place among the future leaders. Only an in-depth inquiry in his home town of Loches could throw some light on this rare and precocious meteor.

Almost everything is known about Henri Desgrange, his intellectual ability, his insatiable desire to work hard and.... his pigheadedness. After having given up, he quickly changed his mind and continued to refine his Tour de France to make it into the institution which we now know. His love of sport and his personal search for eternal youth pushed him to exercise his old body. In a patriotic fashion, he expounded with authority between the wars on the defense of the country. Up unti the end, when due to the censors bland white spaces appeared in the pages of *L'Auto,* he used his pen to exalt people to continue the struggle. Then he died. It was the 16th of August, 1940. The sun shone on Beauvallon, his villa on the Cote d'Azur.

Géo Lefèvre. The gentle Géo. Curiously, the Tour de France 1904, which he directed with his youthful energy and his blossoming authority, was to be the last one for him. Desgrange steered him towards the automobile, then towards aviation and rugby. His smooth and lyrical pen produced other literary masterpieces. Guess who replaced him as cycling editor? Charles Ravaud, his acidic rival of the defunct *Le Velo.* The year 1961 wrenched him from his friends. He was 84.

Georges Abran. A supporting actor? A mere enforcer of managerial decrees? But certainly a key figure and one of the most picturesque. In spite of the mistakes over the direction arrows for which he had been called to account by the boss, he did not leave the Tour de France. It needed the 1914 war to tear this elegant veteran away from "his" Tour. The year 1918 saw the final disappearance of this engaging man.

These leading figures disappeared. We have followed them, full of vitality, to the heart of the events of 1904, and briefly rediscovered them again towards the end of their lives, in other circumstances. The Tour de France always turns towards the present. The bikes are still built around their wheels. There are no longer any "disinherited" ones among the riders, even though some of them sometimes wonder. Horses are no longer to be seen on the roads, the straw hats and long dresses have left the pavements. But the riders still need the same things - a big heart and a lot of courage. Long live the bicycle and the beautiful epic of the Tour de France, image of the eternal adventure!

1904 List of Starting Riders

Achten, Joseph (Bel) DNF
Aucouturier, Hippolyte (Fra) DQ
Beaugendre, Francois (Fra) *
Blanqui, Adrien (Fra) DNF
Boyer, Felix (Fra) DNF
Boyer, H. (Fra) DNF
Brange, Eugene (Fra) DNF
Carrère, Maurice (Fra) DNF
Chaput, _____ (Fra) DNF
Chevalier, _____ (Fra) DNF
Catteau, Alois (Bel) DNF
Cist, _____ (Fra) DNF
Cnops, Pierre (Bel) DNF
Colas, _____ (Fra) DNF
Colsaet, Louis (Bel) 7th Place
Cornet, Henri (Fra) 1st Place **
Damelincourt, _____ (Fra) 14th Place
Dargassies, Jean (Fra) 4th Place
Dartigue, Maurice (Fra) DNF
Daumain, _____ (Fra) DNF
Debalade, Philippe (Fra) DNF
Deflotiere, Antoine (Fra) 15th Place
Desuages, Pierre (Fra) DNF
Deveze, Victor (Fra) DNF
Dome, _____ (Bel) DNF
Dortignacq, Jean-Baptiste (Fra) 2nd Place
Doury, Octave (Fra) DNF
Drioul, Gustave (Fra) 10th Place
Dufraix, P. (Fra) DNF
Durant, _____ Fra) DNF
Faure, Antoine (Fra) DNF
Filly, Camille (Fra) DNF
Fleury, Georges (Fra) DNF
Frederic, Michel (Fra) DNF
Gabory, Julien (Fra) DNF
Garin, Cèsar (Fra) DQ
Garin, Maurice (Fra) DQ
Gauban, Henri (Fra) DNF

Gauthier, _____ (Fra) 12th Place
Geay, Eugene (Fra) DNF
Gerbi, Giovanni (Ita) DNF
Grimenwald, _____ (Fra) DNF
Habets, Leon (Fra) DNF
Hibon, P. (Fra) DNF
Jacquet, Jean-Baptiste (Fra) DNF
Jaeck, Albert (Sui) DNF
Jamar, Dieudonne (Bel) DNF
Jousselin, Philippe (Fra) DNF
Laeser, Charles (Sui) DNF
Lambeuf, _____ (Fra) DNF
Lamouline, _____ (Fra) DNF
LaPree, _____ (Fra) DNF
Lardillier, Romain (Fra) DNF
Lecuona, Louis (Fra) DNF
Legaux, _____ (Fra) DNF
Leroy, Albert (Fra) DNF
Lipman, _____ (Fra) DNF
Lombard, Emile (Bel) DNF
Maisoneuve (Fra) DNF
Maitron, Julieu (Fra) 5th Place
Marcastel, _____ (Fra) DNF
Memo, _____ (Bel) DNF
Monin, _____ (Fra) DNF
Moulin, Emile (Fra) DNF
Niepceron, Albert (Fra) DNF
Paret, Henri (Fra) 11th Place
Payan, Ferdinand (Fra) DNF
Pillon, Edouard (Fra) DNF
Pothier, Lucien (Fra) DQ
Poupin, Emile (Fra) DNF
Prèvost, Charles (Fra) DNF
Prèvost, Eugene (Fra) DNF
Prèvost, Noel (Fra) DNF
Priem, Cees (Ned) DNF
Reidenbach, _____ (Fra) DNF
Riche, Leon (Fra) DNF
Rist, Albert (Fra) 13th Place
Rossisignoli, Giovanni (Itl) DNF

Saget, _____ (Fra) 9th Place
Sales, Jules (Bel) DNF
Samson, Julien (Bel) DNF - given name is Julien Lootens
Serres, Georges (Fra) DNS
Sylvain, _____ (Fra) DNF
Tachet, _____ (Fra) DNF
Treuvelot, L. (Fra) DNF
Varalde, Ange (Fra) DNF
Vassela, _____ (Fra) DNF
Ventresque, Eugene (Fra) DNF

88 Total Riders

DNS - Did Not Start
DNF - Did Not Finish
DQ - Disqualified

Bel - Belgium
Fra - France
Itl - Italy
Sui - Switzerland
Ned - Netherlands

Appendix

Official Communique of the U.V.F.

Decisions

The sporting commission of the Union Velocipedique de France, meeting in Paris, at the headquarters of the Union Velocipedique de France, 6 Boulevard des Italiens, under the presidency of Mr. Leon Breton, the 30th November, 1904.

Considering:

(1) That the commissioners of the Tour de France race of 1904 have transmitted to the Sporting Commission, on the date of the 1st of August, 1904, the following statement:

Statement

The commissioners of the Tour de France race, Messrs. Hesse, Gatoux and Levasseur, met on the 1st of August in the office of *L'Auto*, in order to take note of the various complaints lodged by the competitors or by the controllers of the race. They decided:

(1) To reject the complaint from the rider Dortignacq concerning his classification at the finish of the second stage, Lyon-Marseille, the decision of the judge at the finish line is final and without appeal;

(2) To reduce to 100F, the maximum figure allowed by the U.V.F. for race commissioners to fine riders during a race, the fines of 300F inflicted on Pothier and Aucouturier for infractions of the rules on the first stage;

(3) To sanction the removal from the race of Chevallier in the first stage, and of Payan in the second, for a serious infraction of the rules;

(4) To send back the other complaints to the Sporting Commission of the U.V.F., who alone will be able to proceed with the complaints and listen to the riders in question.

Paris, August 1, 1904

Signed: Hesse, Gatoux, Levasseur.

(2) That it has remitted with the above statements from the organizers of the race, two files of complaints divided into nine sections which have been received. Sections 1, 2, and 3 are placed together. Sections 4, 5, 6, 7, and 8 are devoted to the first, second, third, fourth and sixth stages of the Tour de France, and contain a number of claims set out in the general section. Section 9 is exclusively devoted to Dortignacq.

Expects that:

1) That the Tour de France race was run according to the race rules of the U.V.F. and that an organizer's license was delivered to the organizing newspaper, *L'Auto*;

2) That as well, and as it has the right, special rules were drawn up by the organizers, these rules being printed in the form of a bulletin, contained 27 articles, which were read and approved by each of the riders engaged in the Tour de France;

3) That after a long enquiry into the subject of complaints lodged against 29 riders, all have been summoned and listened to by the Sporting Commission, as well as a large number of witnesses, this being in line with the rules of racing, except for those who had no wish to reply to the request which had been addressed to them;

4) That after examining all of these reprehensible cases which were submitted, that besides all these noted criminal acts, many others were committed by riders who, unfortunately remain unpunished, due to insufficient proof.

Declares that:

(1) That it reaffirms the statements made when judging the frauds committed during the Bordeaux-Paris race and that authorization of events organized on the basis of the Tour de France, will be given as rarely as possible;

(2) In future road events, we will act with even more severity in order to stop the considerable harm which has so far been

done to cycling sport.

With these declarations in mind, the Sporting Commission give as their final judgement:

A. On the decision of the commissioners of the Tour de France race,

Decides that:

(1) To confirm the decision taken regarding the rider Dortignacq;
(2) To invalidate the fines inflicted on the riders Aucouturier and Dortignacq, these fines being redundant with the penalties indicated elsewhere;
(3) To confirm the decisions taken with regard to Chevallier and Payon.

B. On the enquiry conducted by the Sporting Commission at the request of the race commissioners,

Decides that:

(1) For being in breach of the articles 6 and 7 of the special rules of the Tour de France race, the following riders are excluded from the race:

From the total route, Aucouturier, César Garin, Maurice Garin, Pothier.
For the first stage: Jousselin, Payan, Prévost, Samson.
For the second stage: Payan
For the fifth stage: Prévost.

(2) For being in breach of articles 9, 11 and 12 of the special rules of the Tour de France race, the following riders are excluded from the race:
For the second stage: Filly
For the third stage: Filly
For the fourth stage: Filly
For the fifth stage: de Baladé, Carrére, Chaput, Filly, Geay.

For the sixth stage: de Baladé, Carrére, Chaput, Delaye, Filly, Geay.

(3) For being in breach of articles 5 and 8 of the special rules of the Tour de France and for generally being in breach of the race rules of the Union Velocipedique de France, the following penalties are inflicted:

a. A warning is addressed to the following riders: Cornet, Dortignacq.

b. A warning is addressed and a reprimand is inflicted on the following rider: Aucouturier.

c. The following riders are expelled from the race:
   1) From the whole route: Chaput
   2) From the first stage: Chevallier.

d. The following riders are suspended:
   Chaput: for life
   Chevallier: for life
   Pothier: for life;
   Maurice Garin: for two years;
   Payan: for one year
   Prévost: for one year.

Classification of the Riders

As a consequence of the rulings, the classifications were established as follows:

1st Stage -- Paris - Lyon
1. Frederick, won 750 F
2. Gerbi, won 350 F
3. Beaugendre, won 175 F
4. Lombard, won 100 F
5. Gauban, won 50 F
6. Faure, won 50 F
7. Gabory, won 25 F
8. Cornet, won 25 F

2nd Stage -- Lyon - Marseille
1. Faure, won 500 F
2. Lombard, won 225 F
3. Cornet, won 100 F
4. Dortignacq, won 75 F
5. Catteau, won 50 F
6. Gabory, won 50 F
7. Samson, won 25 F
8. Ventresque, won 25 F

3rd Stage -- Marseille - Toulouse
1. Cornet, won 400 F
2. Beaugendre, won 175 F
3. Dortignacq, won 100 F
4. Catteau, won 75 F
5. Jousselin, won 50 F
6. Dargassies, won 25 F
7. Carrère, won 25 F
8. Faure, won 25 F

4th Stage -- Toulouse - Bordeaux
1. Beaugendre, won 350 F
2. Jousselin, won 150 F
3. Cornet, won 100 F
4. Maitron, won 50 F

5. Catteau, won 25 F
6. Gabory, won 25 F
7. Dortignac, won 25 F

5th Stage -- Bordeaux - Nantes

1. Dortignac, won 400 F
2. Cornet, won 250 F
3. Jousselin, won 125 F
4. Gabory, won 75 F
5. Daumain, won 50 F
6. Colsaet, won 25 F
7. Damelincourt, won 25 F

6th Stage -- Nantes - Paris

Classement general

1. Cornet - won 5000 F
2. Dortignac, won 3000 F
3. Catteau, won 1500 F
4. Dargassies, won 1000 F
5. Maitron, won 500 F
6. Daumain, won 400 F
7. Colsaet, won 300 F
8. Colas, won 200 F
9. Saget, won 100 F
10. Drioul, won 100 F
11. Paret, won 100 F
12. Gautier, won 100 F
13. Rist, won 100 F
14. Damelincourt, won 100 F
15. De Flotrière, won 100 F

Consultations

L'Auto 1904
Le Velo, 1904
Le Journal de l'Automobile, 1904
La Vie au Grand Air, 1904
Le Cycliste, 1904
La Bicyclette, 1895
Le Cycle, 1895
Le Veloce-Sport, 1895
Les Champions du cycle (A. Marrel), 1903
Cinq annees du Tour de France (G. Abran et Ch. Ravaud), 1908
Le Dictionnaire cycliste (P. Beving), 1922
Ceux que j'ai connus (Geo Lefèvre), 1962
Et les archives Jacques Seray.